The Persuasive Power
of Campaign Advertising

The
Persuasive Power
of Campaign
Advertising

Travis N. Ridout
Michael M. Franz

TEMPLE UNIVERSITY PRESS
Philadelphia

TEMPLE UNIVERSITY PRESS
Philadelphia, Pennsylvania 19122
www.temple.edu/tempress

Library of Congress Cataloging-in-Publication Data

Ridout, Travis N., 1974–
    The persuasive power of campaign advertising / Travis N. Ridout
and Michael M. Franz.
        p.   cm.
    Includes bibliographical references.
    ISBN 978-1-4399-0332-2 (hardcover : alk. paper)
    ISBN 978-1-4399-0333-9 (pbk. : alk. paper)
    ISBN 978-1-4399-0334-6 (e-book)
    1. Political campaigns—United States.   2. Advertising, Political—
United States.   I. Franz, Michael M., 1976–   II. Title.

    JK2281.R54 2011
    324.7'30973—dc22   2010035516

♾ The paper used in this publication meets the requirements of the
American National Standard for Information Sciences—Permanence
of Paper for Printed Library Materials, ANSI Z39.48-1992

Printed in the United States of America

2 4 6 8 9 7 5 3 1

 # Contents

Preface   vii

1   The Role of Campaign Advertising   1

2   The Problem of Persuasion   21

3   A Brief Primer on Data and Research Design   37

4   How Race Context Matters   51

5   How Negativity and Emotional Appeals in Ads Matter   79

6   How Receivers' Characteristics Matter   103

7   How Ad Coverage in News Matters   133

8   The Future Study of Ad Effects   145

Appendix A: Variable Coding   153

Appendix B: Full Model Results from Chapter 4   161

Appendix C: Additional Model Results from Chapter 5   169

References   171

Index   181

Preface

THIS BOOK BEGAN as an idea in 2004 while working with
Paul Freedman and Ken Goldstein on *Campaign Advertising
and American Democracy* (Temple, 2007). In the first drafts of
that book, we considered including some discussion of ads' effects on
voters' candidate preferences. As we fleshed out the idea and wrote
some prose, however, we knew that the concept deserved its own
lengthy treatment. There were too many interesting questions that
deserved specific attention. What kinds of ads are most persuasive?
Who is more strongly affected by ad exposure? How does the coverage
of ads in local news affect the persuasive properties of the ads? Because
so many interesting questions entered these initial discussions, we sat
down after the publication of the earlier book and drafted an outline.
The resulting book does not address or answer all of the potential factors that condition ad persuasion—that would take a much longer
analysis and probably more than one volume—but it does tackle the
major questions asked by scholars, journalists, and citizens.

In between that initial outline and now, three federal elections have
taken place: the congressional elections of 2006 and 2010 and the presidential election of 2008. Such is the case with scholarship on American campaigns: another election is always around the corner, with
new technologies and tactical innovations changing the landscape.

We have worked to include some discussion of the 2006 and 2008 elections in this book (including modeling ad effects in those years) and the subsequent spread of Internet advertising, but we do not think the empirical analysis is all that sensitive to the inclusion or exclusion of election years. The research herein shows that ads work, and they work in a lot of circumstances. We demonstrate this in presidential and Senate elections across years and surveys. We think the results are robust and the conclusions, general.

Moreover, it seems unlikely that political advertising is waning as a method of reaching voters. Some preliminary numbers from 2010 reinforce a point we make strongly in Chapter 1. For example, in September and October of 2008, over 400,000 ads were aired nationally advocating for U.S. House candidates. In the just-completed 2010 elections, ad volume in House races jumped to over 620,000 ads aired, an increase of 46 percent. In Senate races, the volume of ads aired in the fall campaign increased by 12 percent over 2008, from 440,000 ads to just under 500,000 ads. These increases were not attributable to just one type of sponsor. Candidates, parties, and independent groups all bought more ads in 2010 than in 2008. In total there were more ads aired in the 2010 congressional elections than in any previous set of congressional elections for which there are data. Ads are as dominant as ever, and they surely will continue to play a key role in the coming 2012 presidential election.

A lot of people ask us whether ads matter, and, of course, the answer depends. But, in general, we can say confidently that ads are persuasive, especially if you have more ads than your competitor. This does not mean that money to buy ads determines electoral success, however. That is the importance of the empirical work in this book. Many ads fall flat, but when they do so depends in part on the context of the race, the characteristics of the ads, and the profile of the viewer.

MANY PEOPLE deserve special thanks as we complete this work. Bowdoin College and its junior leave policy helped Michael Franz devote the 2008–2009 academic year to completing a draft and working on revisions. A Faculty Research Award also helped fund a trip to Washington, D.C., in spring 2009 to discuss electoral innovations with political consultants. Thanks, in particular, go to Joel Rivlin and Frank Chi for taking the time to discuss ads, the Internet, and micro-targeting. Mike's colleagues in the Government Department were also very helpful, creating an atmosphere in which an assistant professor could devote a lot of time to research and writing. Moreover, his students were more than eager to discuss advertising and its likely impact on the political process. Steve Smith was an incredible research assistant in the summer of 2007. He ably coded hundreds of ads on emotional content and offered good advice to streamline and improve the coding. Students in Mike's Campaigns and Elections class in fall 2007 helped with inter-coder reliability, and more than a few students wondered how the coding of ads on emotional content could be enhanced. Mike's wife, Laura, was a strong advocate of the book, urging him to consider specific changes in the narrative and analysis. She thoroughly enjoyed the trips to Washington in spring 2009 and happily wandered the halls of the Smithsonian as Mike learned more about ad targeting from practitioners. As the book was completed, Mike welcomed his son Charlie into the world, a true gift.

Travis Ridout thanks Jenny Holland for her work as a coder on this project and thanks his colleagues at Washington State University for their support of his research, whether offering helpful advice or just leaving him alone in his office to write. He also thanks his wife, Carolyn, for her unwavering support and for giving him two wonderful daughters, Lorelei and Julianne, during the course of writing this book.

We also thank Ken Goldstein for granting us access to the advertising data in 2000, 2004, 2006, and 2008. As we write, both of us have taken on the advertising project in collaboration with Erika Franklin Fowler at Wesleyan University. The Wisconsin Advertising Project has now become the Wesleyan Media Project, and we are excited to work with Erika. Her feedback on some analysis here was incredibly helpful, especially with the data on local news coverage of ads in Chapter 7.

The anonymous reviewers of this draft offered first-rate feedback, and there is little doubt that the book is far better because of their analysis. Alex Holzman was a wonderful guide, and we are very grateful to go through the publication process yet again under his wise counsel.

NOT MANY PEOPLE love political ads, and many people question whether they help or harm American democracy. Our hope is that this book contributes to that important debate and provides readers with some valuable answers.

The Persuasive Power
of Campaign Advertising

The Role of
Campaign Advertising

DURING EVERY election campaign, American politicians invade our television sets. They enter our lives uninvited and in thirty-second increments. We see them during commercial breaks while watching our favorite talk or game shows. We see them between the sports and weather updates during the local news. We might even see them before a television judge renders a verdict on a case, or during a rerun of a law or medical drama on cable television.

These political messages come in many shades and tones. Some of them are positive and uplifting, where candidates recount the struggles and triumphs of their lives. Many evoke feelings of enthusiasm, hope, or joy, cued with a crescendo of uplifting music. Some show the American flag waving. Others depict the candidate eagerly talking with everyday Americans about economic or moral issues.

Some ads, by contrast, are negative and nasty, attacking an opponent's policy ideas or personal character. Many of these messages try to scare or anger us, using ominous music or unflattering black-and-white photos of a political opponent. The point of these ads is crystal clear: your future depends on my election to office.

Not all ads are sponsored by candidates, of course. The Democratic and Republican parties are major players in the advertising game.

Some of their ads are coordinated with candidates' campaigns, and some are produced and aired independently. Outside interest groups are also part of the mix. Labor unions are perennially present, for example, but increasingly so are groups with strange-sounding names: Americans for Job Security, Freedom's Watch, Majority Action, Vets for Freedom, and American Rights at Work.

In short, televised political advertising is everywhere, and its ubiquity raises fundamental questions. Does any of it really matter? Do political ads break through the clutter and enter the consciousness of the American voter? In other words, do they influence citizens' views of the candidates and affect how they vote on Election Day? On the one hand, of course, the answer seems obvious. They must matter. Why, otherwise, would candidates and their allies spend so much money on them?

This is certainly the impression that one gains from journalistic coverage of campaigns. For example, Tom Wicker wrote in the *New York Times* in 1988 that many blamed the Democratic presidential candidate Michael Dukakis's loss on "Willie Horton . . . rather than [the success of] ideological conservatism" (Wicker 1988). The Willie Horton ads were some of the most famous political ads of the previous thirty years, and they attempted to depict Dukakis as soft on crime (Geer 2006, 121–123; Mendelberg 2001).

Many believe it was a few ads by the organization Swift Boat Veterans for Truth, featuring men who had served with John Kerry in Vietnam, that led to Kerry's loss in 2004. As the veteran journalist Robert Novak put it on an appearance on *Meet the Press* in July 2007, "For Republicans [in 2004] a swift boat was a very good thing. [It] kept John Kerry from being president."[1]

And it was Hillary Clinton's "3 A.M." ad, asking which Democratic candidate voters would want answering the phone at the time of a national crisis, that propelled her to victory in Pennsylvania during the 2008 nominating contest—at least according to some. Mark Penn, Clinton's chief strategist, had this to say about the ad in August 2008: "Clever negative advertising works. That is reality. The tactic meets

---

[1] Transcript, MSNBC.com, July 15, 2007, available online at http://www.msnbc.msn.com/id/19694666/print/1/displaymode/1098 (accessed January 29, 2010).

with media and pundit disapproval and spawns accusations of negativity, but the reality is that a clever negative ad can be devastatingly effective."[2]

Although there is some scholarly evidence that political commercials move votes, there is still no consensus about the extent of advertising's impact—that is, how many votes, if any, are changed. Many scholars have chosen to investigate important *byproduct* effects of advertising, such as the relationship between advertising tone and citizens' involvement or participation in the political system. But as Huber and Arceneaux (2007, 957) write, "Few studies that analyze actual campaigns have been able to demonstrate that advertisements persuade individuals to change their minds."

Much political-science research more generally would suggest that ads should have little impact on changing people's candidate preferences. Many people enter election campaigns as partisans, for example, which makes it difficult to sway these voters. Moreover, scholars have shown that election outcomes can be predicted quite well on the basis of a few pieces of data known months before an election—indeed, months before the bulk of advertising has been aired (Holbrook 1996).[3] Other scholars submit that while advertising might have the potential to sway voters when one side dominates the airwaves, most presidential campaigns are balanced ones in which competing messages cancel each other out (Zaller 1996).

And consider this: if you ask typical Americans what they think of negative campaign ads they see on television, many will tell you that they detract from American politics—that they weaken democratic discourse (see Geer 2006, 2). For example, in a 2006 Gallup poll, 69 percent of Americans reported that they believe little or nothing of what is said in political advertising. Further, opinion poll after opinion poll finds that Americans think politics and campaigns are too negative. In 2006, for example, 63 percent of respondents in a different national poll reported that Republican candidates' ads were

---

[2] Quoted in Politico.com, August 11, 2008, available online at http://www.politico.com/news/stories/0808/12455.html (accessed January 29, 2010).

[3] Indeed, scholars in political science have debated for years the existence and magnitude of campaign and media effects: see Holbrook 1996, chap. 1; Johnston, Hagen, and Jamieson 2004.

"too negative"; 61 percent reported that ads from Democratic candidates were "too negative." Nearly 70 percent reported that neither Democratic nor Republican ads "provided useful information."[4] If Americans do not trust political ads, then how can they persuade?

What emerges is a compelling puzzle. Even as campaigns spend lots of money on television ads, believing that they are crucial for victory, some scholars believe their effects are small, and many citizens express displeasure at their abundance. Our goal in this book is to offer the most comprehensive examination to date of the persuasive power of televised campaign ads. In other words, we hope to offer a more definitive answer to the enduring questions of how, when, and whether ads matter. We should be clear at the outset. The intended audience for this book is broad—students of American politics, journalists, political consultants, and interested citizens. As we make clear later, our primary contribution is not theoretical. In fact, we use the rich existing scholarship on campaign effects to lay out a number of commonly understood expectations about the effectiveness of political advertising. To these expectations we bring to bear the best data available and a sophisticated methodological approach. This methodological advance is our primary contribution.

More specifically, the book examines advertising in American election campaigns in 2000 and 2004, focusing in both years on the presidential elections and sixty Senate races. We also add in a later chapter a discussion of Senate advertising in 2006, and we include a preliminary analysis of persuasion effects at the county level in the presidential and Senate races of 2008. We do all of this by focusing on citizens' exposure to the *complete* ad environment in a campaign. Because of that, we say very little about the impact of specific ads. Indeed, as avid consumers of American politics, and as scholars in the field, we are often asked to reflect on the effectiveness of certain ads. Did Mike Huckabee's "Chuck Norris" ad help him win the Iowa caucuses in January 2008? Did John McCain's ad in the summer of 2008, which featured images of Paris Hilton and Britney Spears, lead citizens to dismiss Barack Obama as little more than a celebrity? We wish,

---

[4] The first poll was conducted in October 2006 by *USA Today* and the Gallup Organization; the second was sponsored by *Newsweek* the same month.

of course, that we could provide rock-solid evidence about the effectiveness of the latest and most discussed campaign ads—and make predictions about their effectiveness as soon as they appear. We could make millions as media consultants if such questions could be answered prospectively and definitively.

Ultimately, however, an in-depth focus on one or two ads in a campaign would only begin to answer the question of how the ad environment in total influences citizens' attitudes and choices. Indeed, most citizens in actual campaigns view multiple political ads and often in high numbers. Isolating the effect of one or a few viewings of one or a few ads would miss the total impact of advertising in any particular campaign.

Our contention in this book is relatively simple, actually. We argue that campaign ads *do* matter, but their impact is largely contingent. More specifically, we focus on the influence of television ads as moderated by three key factors: the characteristics of the ads (promotional versus attack ads, for example), the campaign context in which they air (such as open seats and competitive races with an incumbent running), and the receiver of the ad message (partisan viewers or independent viewers, to name two). These are not the only conditions under which an ad's effectiveness might be moderated, of course; the issues discussed in the ads may help or hinder a campaign's persuasive appeals; the presence or absence of a scandal may also matter, as might the overall production quality of the ads. The three major factors that we focus on here, however, are the ones scholars have studied the most and are arguably the most important factors that condition the influence of advertising.

Determining the actual persuasive influence of campaign advertising is more than an academic exercise, however. Such an investigation matters for any evaluation of contemporary American politics. Indeed, elections are the primary means by which voters and their elected representatives are connected, and political advertising in particular accounts for the overwhelming bulk of candidates' and parties' electioneering budgets. Voters are often bombarded by these short messages, and in many cases they represent the voter's only exposure to the candidate. This is particularly true for political novices who may avoid news media or Internet blog coverage of campaigns.

If ads aired during an election campaign do, in fact, alter voters' candidate preferences, determining the if and when is only part of the bigger story. We must also ask *how* ads are persuading. On the one hand, ads might be "manipulating," convincing people to vote for a candidate who might act against their best interests. This would be quite troublesome, as it would suggest that the candidate who has the most money to buy ads will be the victor, not the candidate who is more representative of the particular electorate.

On the other hand, ads might be persuading by informing, by providing people with the information that they need to make enlightened decisions about which candidates best represent their interests. In this case, ads are not troublesome but represent one more way by which to bring information to voters, offering a connection between elector and elected.[5]

The Relevance of Television Advertising

It is likely true that the Internet is the next wave of electioneering innovation, and it may someday supplant television as the primary method of reaching voters—we can hardly deny these developments. For example, in their seminal study of young voters in contemporary American politics, Winograd and Hais (2008, 154) argue that "[Internet politics] present the possibility of an end to the ever rising cost of thirty-second television campaign commercials, and the time-consuming and potentially corrupting need to raise the money to pay for them." The development of sophisticated online outreach technology, they add, "will cause television to lose its role as the primary medium for campaigns to get their messages out to voters in the near future" (Winograd and Hais 2008, 163). Given such claims, is it even worth studying the effects of televised advertising? Are we exploring a "dying art"?

---

[5] Indeed, there is a rich scholarship in political science on the ability of voters to make informed decisions on the basis of minimal information (Downs 1957; Sniderman, Brody, and Tetlock 1991). It seems reasonable to suggest that campaign advertising is one source of information voters can use to make short-term and quick judgments about candidates (Franz, Freedman, Goldstein, and Ridout 2007, 12–18). The usefulness of ads, however, is predicated on the likelihood that they will not draw voters away from candidates they would normally be predisposed to support.

Our answer is emphatic. We believe it *is* important to study political advertising on television, largely because the immediate impact of the Internet (now and in the foreseeable future) is a transformation in how candidates and their political allies fund advertising, not in how they attempt to persuade voters. Even the most recent studies of the effects of digital media in elections agree. For example, according to Kate Kaye (2009, 14, 19), "Many political consultants don't think Internet ads can be used to sway voters. . . . Obama grabbed millions of dollars through online fundraising from countless donors giving relatively small amounts of cash. But, as in every election in recent history, the bulk of that money was spent on television ads." Simply put, the Internet as superior campaign communicator is not yet here.

This leaves television—still—as the primary medium for reaching potential voters. This is true even at a time when campaigns are keenly aware of the fragmentation of the American media. That is, with the proliferation of cable news choices, Americans have ever more abundant options in news and entertainment. This transition from a "broadcast" media environment, where Americans have only a few channels and popular programs have huge audiences, to a "narrowcast" media, where audience share is split up over hundreds of programs, leaves television advertisements potentially struggling to break through to potential voters. As Martin Wattenberg (2010, 57) has noted, viewership for major presidential speeches and press conferences is down significantly, by as much as 50 percent for the State of the Union between 1980 and 2005.

A recent U.S. Supreme Court decision may even make televised political advertising more prominent in the future. The court ruled in early 2010 that corporations and unions were free to spend unlimited amounts of money on advertising that directly advocated the election or defeat of a candidate, a practice that was previously illegal at the federal level and in many states. Some predict this will make political ads even more prevalent. The preliminary evidence from 2010 bears this out, in fact, as we noted in the Preface.

Moreover, people are not abandoning their television sets, despite other entertainment options. In November 2009, Nielsen reported that the average household was watching more television each day (more than eight hours) than in any previous period, up 11 percent from 1999.[6] Even when Americans watch shows recorded on digital video recorders (DVRs), a substantial proportion (nearly half, according to some estimates) watch the recorded commercials instead of fast-forwarding through them (Carter 2009). David Carr of the *New York Times* had this to say in May 2009:

> Why, as network television has been sliced in half in terms of audience in the last few decades, do marketers still buy in? First and foremost, because it works. At a time of ever-atomizing audiences, broadcast television's slice may be smaller, but it is still the biggest slice. Think network television is washed up, overwhelmed by targeted and measureable ads on the Web? How is it that Apple, a tech company, and by the way, probably the most talented marketing company on the planet, is all over network television right now? And remember the movie industry is having a big year with big movies, using, yes, network television to drive people into theaters. Network television advertising retains traction with both buyers and consumers because, in spite of the proliferation of screens, people are still watching more television than ever. (Carr 2009)

Campaigns clearly recognize this, since the volume of paid televised political advertising has remained relatively stable across recent election cycles, as data from the Wisconsin Advertising Project reveal.[7] Table 1.1 shows some summary statistics about the number of presidential ads (paid for by either candidates or outside groups) aired in each media market in each of three presidential nomination seasons:

---

[6] Report posted on Nielsen's blog, available online at http://blog.nielsen.com (accessed January 13, 2010). Since 2005, Nielsen's totals for daily household viewing have included shows recorded with a DVR and played back within seven days.

[7] The Wisconsin Advertising Project is housed at the University of Wisconsin, Madison, and is directed by Kenneth Goldstein. As graduate students, we were involved with the collection and coding of the ad data for the 2000 election. More information about the ad data is provided in Chapter 3. Prior to the project's establishment in 1998, data on the frequency of ad airings is only anecdotal, although Shaw (1999) provides some numbers on ad Gross Ratings Points obtained from the presidential campaigns for 1988, 1992 and 1996. The University of Oklahoma maintains an archive of political advertisements back to the 1950s, but the archive has no information on the frequency with which the ads aired.

TABLE 1.1   Number of Ads per Media Market by Year
(Presidential Nomination Races)

Number of ads per media market	1999–2000	2003–2004	2007–2008
Mean	1,349	1,432	1,860
25th percentile	121	318	214
Median	787	989	997
75th percentile	1,569	1,434	2,348

Source: Wisconsin Advertising Project
Note: The period covered is from October 1 of the previous year until the nomination was secured. Ad totals are for the top seventy-five markets in 2000 and for all 210 markets in 2004 and 2008.

1999–2000, 2003–2004, and 2007–2008. A media market is simply a geographic area in which most people have access to similar television and radio broadcasts and newspapers. The number of markets for which we have access to ad-tracking data has increased over time (from the top 75 media markets in 1998 and 2000 to all 210 markets for presidential candidates in 2004 and 2008). To make these numbers comparable over time, we report summary statistics about the number of ads aired in each market, not the total number of ads aired across all markets.

In each successive nomination campaign, the mean and median number of ads increases. To put these figures into perspective, keep in mind that while both Republicans and Democrats were battling for their parties' nominations in 2000, only Democrats had a contested race in 2004. And in spite of that, there was a substantial increase in total advertising between those two years. Part of the increase in 2007–2008 could be due to the unusually long race on the Democratic side, but the market-level summaries that we report should not be very sensitive to the length of the nominating contest. With the exception of Iowa and New Hampshire, which saw campaigning and advertising for most of 2007, most markets in the primary phase of the presidential election received high advertising volumes right before their primary or caucus date and very little right after.

In sum, it seems clear that the volume of advertising has increased in presidential nomination races in recent years. Why? The most likely explanation for this has to do with changes in campaign-finance law and changes in the ways in which candidates have gone about soliciting donations. First, after the 2002 elections, the limit on an individual contribution to a candidate rose from $1,000 to $2,000, making it easier for candidates to raise funds from relatively wealthy donors.[8] But at the same time, a ban on large unregulated contributions to political parties, which began after the 2002 elections, compelled the parties and individual campaigns to reach out to heretofore untapped millions of small-money donors—done largely on the Internet.

This is perhaps best exemplified by Howard Dean's campaign for the Democratic presidential nomination in 2004, which was able to raise $52 million through Internet contributions (Hindman 2005). In 2008, Barack Obama raised, by some estimates, more than $300 million for the primary campaign, with up to $200 million coming from Internet contributions (http://www.cfinst.org). The ability to raise large sums of cash for the primary campaign has convinced many presidential primary candidates in recent years to forgo the public funding option, whereby the government matches private contributions to a candidate in exchange for the candidate's promise to limit spending in primary states. This has consequently raised the amounts of money spent on the nominating contest and resulted in greater use of televised political advertising.

Does this trend of rising ad airings hold for other races, however? To examine this, we calculated the number of congressional ads aired per market in 1998, 2000, 2002, 2004, and 2008, including all U.S. Senate and U.S. House races (Table 1.2). The evidence is compelling. There was a substantial increase in coverage between 1998 and 2000, and while the amount of advertising in 2002, 2004, and 2008 seemed to plateau (and even decline in a few categories), all three years saw substantially higher levels of advertisements over 1998.

The initial bump in the volume of advertising between 1998 and 2000 is perhaps best explained by the changing sponsorship of ads. Around 1998, outside groups and parties began paying for increased levels of television advertising, a trend that has continued in recent years. The reasoning for this was a much more partisan and polarized political environment in Washington after 1994 (making every com-

---

[8] The $2,000 figure is also indexed to inflation. Thus, the individual upper limit was $2,100 in 2006, $2,300 in 2008, and $2,400 in 2010.

TABLE 1.2 Number of Ads per Media Market by Year (House and Senate)

Number of ads per media market	1998	2000	2002	2004	2008
Mean	4,096	6,496	5,967	5,568	5,852
25th percentile	1,164	2,374	1,842	1,639	1,135
Median	2,620	5,902	4,821	4,189	4,153
75th percentile	6,592	9,540	9,113	7,946	7,749

Source: Wisconsin Advertising Project

Note: Ad totals are for the top seventy-five markets in 1998 and 2000, the top one hundred markets in 2002 and 2004, and all 210 markets in 2008.

petitive House and Senate election crucial to liberal and conservative interests), coupled with far looser restrictions on how ads could be funded (Franz 2008). As a consequence, many more political players have chosen to air television ads in the past ten years with the intention of reaching persuadable voters.

For general election presidential advertising between 2000 and 2008, the story is similar (Table 1.3). While the average media market received 4,075 ads in 2000, the number was about 25 percent higher (5,069) in 2004. Note, however, the very small number of ads aired (just three spots) at the 25th percentile. This much wider distribution of ads buys in 2004 is an artifact of the available data. In 2000, we have only ads aired in the top seventy-five markets, but we have ads aired in all 210 markets in 2004. With this complete set of market-level

TABLE 1.3 Number of Ads per Media Market by Year (Presidential General Election)

Number of ads per media market	2000	2004	2008
Mean	4,075	5,069	4,078
25th percentile	1,222	3	5
Median	3,438	717	1,000
75th percentile	6,783	9,509	7,690

Source: Wisconsin Advertising Project

Note: In 2000, we identify the general election as beginning on June 1. In 2004, because John Kerry had secured enough delegates after Super Tuesday, we count March 3 as the beginning of the general election. June 15 is the start point for 2008. Ad totals are for the top seventy-five markets in 2000 and for all 210 markets in 2004 and 2008.

data, we can see that presidential candidates often put a very small number of ads in minor markets.

While advertising surged in 2004, it did decline somewhat in 2008. The average number of ads aired in the top 210 markets during the general election presidential campaign was 4,078. Only the median number of ads was higher that year (1,000 ads in 2008, compared with 717 in 2004). This lower total advertising is the consequence of little interest group advertising in the general election in 2008 (Kimball 2009) and a much lower investment from the Democratic Party, which aired only 7,800 ads in the entire general election phase across all 210 markets. This latter decline was driven by the aggressive fundraising of Barack Obama, who was the first major party nominee to opt out of the general election public funding program.

Our core message here is simply put: the best available evidence suggests that the volume of advertising has increased over recent years or, at least, remained steady. Consider this bit of historical context. When McGinnis (1969) was writing about Richard Nixon's use of television in 1968, the medium had not yet been fully embraced by campaign managers. McGinnis specifically chronicled the divisions within the campaign between the "ad people" and the traditional campaign managers.[9] Forty years later, however, no major campaign consultant would counsel a presidential or Senate candidate to wage a serious campaign without a presence on television. In fact, John Kerry's 2004 bid was essentially run by Bob Shrum, a media and campaign advertising consultant.

The dominance of television in political campaigns is still true even at a time when campaigns are becoming more innovative in the tactics they use. For example, a new trend in elections involves the aggressive mining of consumer purchasing data (tracked by credit card companies) to identify relationships between retail preferences and political choices (Hillygus and Shields 2009); the information is subsequently used to instruct get-out-the-vote efforts and peer-to-peer contacts. Republicans employed this tactic aggressively begin-

---

[9] Curiously, in her discussion of the emergence of digital media in the presidential election of 2008, Kaye (2009) chronicles the challenges some online media consultants, especially for the McCain and Clinton campaigns, faced in being taken seriously by more traditional consultants who specialized in offline campaigning.

ning in the 2004 elections (Gertner 2004; Sosnik, Dowd, and Fournier 2006). Put simply, campaign consultants want to know whether conservatives disproportionately purchase domestic beer and subscribe to hunting magazines, whether liberals prefer lattes at Starbucks and give often to charities; and whether moderates prefer American-made to foreign-made cars. They are able to get answers to these and similar questions through extensive polling that looks for trends and relationships between consumer habits and political attitudes. Voter files are subsequently linked to data on individuals that is purchased from credit card companies and, because polling has identified which consumer habits are associated with which political attitudes, these data can be used by campaigns to develop a highly tailored message and send it via phone calls or direct mail only to certain types of consumers/voters. Targeting along these lines can be so precise that a grandmother in apartment 4B might receive a health-care mailing that emphasizes the candidate's efforts to secure the long-term viability of Medicare, while the graduate student in apartment 6C receives the student-loan mailing that outlines the candidate's commitment to affordable education.[10]

Compare this with the relative inefficiency of traditional television advertising. Most ads are aired on local television news broadcasts or talk shows and games shows (Goldstein and Freedman 2002). A certain demographic watches these programs (Rivlin 2008), of course—usually older voters—but the targeting strategy is broader. Your ad will be seen by your base voters, undecided voters, voters of the other party, and lots of non-voters. What you say on television, then, often can be wasted on viewers who will never vote for you, or never vote at all.

In sum, television remains more of a shotgun tactic than a rifle shot, as the overwhelming majority of ads (especially, still, for lower ticket races) are not targeted to specific demographic audiences.

---

[10] In truth, this tactic really is not new. Before television—before the modern campaign more generally—candidates could micro-target different audiences in different states with different speeches (Hillygus and Shields 2009, 154). Candidates might, for example, tell one audience something in one town but something completely different in a different town. This is the original form of micro-targeting that became impossible in the world of multimedia, where such inconsistencies in message are easily identified. The micro-targeting trend of today, then, is really a technological trend.

Ad Persuasion as an Empirical Question

Although campaign advertising on television continues to be relevant (and will be for some time, we suggest), its actual effect on voters is still a relatively open question. Existing research on the persuasiveness of political advertising is abundant but has been hampered by several challenges.

First, experimental lab findings (see, e.g., Ansolabehere and Iyengar 1995; Chang 2001; Kahn and Geer 1994; Meirick 2002; Pinkleton 1997, 1998; Valentino, Hutchings, and Williams 2004) have been important in helping scholars understand the process by which ads might work—that is, change minds—but it is very difficult to make the transition from the laboratory to what happens in the real world of a campaign. Seeing one or two ads in quick succession just is not the same as seeing a multiplicity of ads from various sources over the course of a lengthy political campaign. For example, if participants in an experiment, on average, are 10 percent more likely to vote for a candidate after seeing one of that candidate's ads in a laboratory setting, what does that mean for the individual at the ballot box on Election Day? Does it increase that likelihood by 10 percent, 1 percent, .01 percent, .000001 percent?

To address this drawback of current scholarship, we focus our investigation in the real world. The ad data we employ come from the Wisconsin Advertising Project, which coded commercial data about which ads aired when and where on dozens of different attributes. We have data on literally hundreds of thousands of political ads aired in top media markets for each year, allowing us to track presidential and Senate advertising over the course of the entire campaign season.

For specific analyses of both the 2000 and 2004 elections, we make use of two studies: the two-wave American National Election Study from 2000 and a three-wave study conducted by the University of Wisconsin and Brigham Young University from 2004. In particular, we focus on two outcome variables—people's reported voting choice and their evaluations of the Democratic and Republican candidates. The use of these panel studies (which re-interview the same people at different points in time) not only allows us to speak confidently about causation—that exposure to advertising led voters to cast their ballots a certain way or feel differently about the candidates—but allows us to examine the effectiveness of advertising at different times during a campaign. This represents the most comprehensive examination to date of the persuasive effect of political advertising.

One major advance of our research over previous scholarship on persuasion, then, is methodological. Our empirical work does not lack a theoretical focus, however. Indeed, we draw on the rich literature on campaign effects to lay out a number of expectations as to *when* and *how* advertising matters. All ads are not alike. All campaign environments are not alike. And all message receivers are not alike. We should not expect the same ad to exert the same degree of influence on each person. Thus, we examine how the context of the campaign may influence the effectiveness of a candidate's advertising, focusing in particular on the competitiveness of the race, whether the messages come from the incumbent or the challenger, and whether the ads were aired during a presidential or Senate campaign.

We also explore how the characteristics of the person who received the ad's message influence the ad's ability to move the person's candidate preference. Our focus is on partisanship and levels of information. Theoretically, strong partisans should be less susceptible to ad influence, as they should be anchored by their partisan attachments; independents, by contrast, should be far more persuadable. Moreover, we propose that those who have low levels of political information should be as open to ad influence as those with who have a lot of political information. This expectation runs counter to some models of persuasion that predict that those with low levels of political information are less able to process, understand, and thus accept political messages. We will argue, though, that because political advertising is a campaign message designed specifically to be easy to understand, lower levels of political sophistication should not impede message reception and acceptance.

Research on political advertising has traditionally relied on the simple categorization of ads as positive (promotional) or negative (attack). Such a coding scheme does not do justice to the ways in which ads differ. In this book, we examine not only whether promotional and negative ads differ in their effects but whether ads that draw on different emotions (from anger to fear to enthusiasm) have different effects on voters. This is important because scholars have only begun to examine whether advertising's effectiveness depends on the emotions the ads evoke (see, e.g., Brader 2006), yet there is much theory suggesting that emotions should matter in campaigns (Marcus and MacKuen 1993).

Finally, research on political advertising outside the laboratory has focused solely on voters' exposure to the televised airings of these messages during commercial breaks. Yet people are also exposed to political ads through the news media and increasingly on the Internet. Think of the ad nauseam coverage in the news media of specific campaign ads in different election cycles—for example, the "Wolves as Terrorists" ad in 2004, and the "Obama as Celebrity" ad sponsored by John McCain in 2008. In addition, the news media often discuss political ads in the context of "ad watches," where reporters evaluate the truth of claims made in television ads. Although this is difficult to study empirically, we will make the case that media coverage of advertising may also have the potential to influence voters' choices.

The Role of Campaign Advertising

We should be clear at the outset that our argument in this book is more empirical than normative. We co-wrote a recent book showing that exposure to campaign ads can actually be healthy for politics; we showed, for example, that ads can raise voters' knowledge about campaigns, spur interest in the election, and even foster voter participation (Franz, Freedman, Goldstein, and Ridout 2007; see also Patterson and McClure 1976). But we did not argue that campaign ads should replace more traditional forms of running for office, such as meeting with and canvassing voters, holding town hall discussions with citizens, participating in candidate debates, and holding campaign rallies. We simply believe that ads are less harmful to the electoral process than the conventional wisdom would suggest. Whatever ails American politics, we are convinced that television ads are not the cause.

However, many people still have misgivings about the role television ads play in elections. Many citizens, as we noted above, continue to express frustration at the abundance of political ads. There is also always the potential for ads to confuse voters or misrepresent the truth. It seems that everyone can offer an example of an ad that seemed beyond the pale or simply untrue. This is particularly relevant in discerning the persuasive power of campaign ads. Are ads pushing voters toward or pulling them away from their predispositions? Can ads trick citizens? These are important questions.

Keep in mind, though, that factual misrepresentations are possible in all forms of campaign discourse, whether they are online, on television, or at a town hall meeting—and this has always been true. Because television ads are so publicly broadcast, however, the ability to lie outright is weakened. And any ad from one candidate or party can always be countered with an ad from the opposing candidate or party—this is a particular strength of television compared with other forms of campaigning. In fact, the counterattack strategy was exercised in the 2008 Democratic nomination battle, when Barack Obama responded almost instantly to Hillary Clinton's "3 A.M." ad. The failure to respond, however, was evident in 2004 when John Kerry chose not to air ads countering the Swift Boat attacks.

Furthermore, if the news media are watching, unfair television ads can and should be the focus of their attention. And with every election cycle, fact-checking websites spend considerable time investigating the distortions and misrepresentations in television advertising.[11] All told, the likelihood that complete falsehoods go on the air unvarnished and without rebuttal is quite low.

Many recommendations for campaign reform, however, have focused on the perceived damaging impact of ads. Some have called for a "positive-only" air war. For example, in 2009, North Carolina's Governor Bev Perdue created a task force to explore the viability of an optional public funding system for state elections that would only grant money to participants if they pledged to air positive ads. The chair of the task force, in discussing one of the possible policy proposals, said, "In order to qualify for endowment money, you [would] have to pledge not to mention your opponent, and we may say that you may not engage in advertising that mentions your opponent. This will be a mechanism to discourage negative campaigning and insist on

---

[11] Two in particular are popular at this writing: http://www.factcheck.org and http://www.politifact.com.

issue discussion" ("Reds and Blues" 2009). At the federal level, a key motivation for forcing candidates to "approve" their message was a hope that negativity in campaigns would go down (Franz, Rivlin, and Goldstein 2006, 141–142).

These reform agendas seem motivated by the assumption that ads are harmful, that thirty-second ads cannot possibly be good for democracy. Thus, the debate over political advertising is an ideal place for political science to make an important contribution to a real-life policy debate. In the chapters that follow, we look for evidence about how often and when persuasion happens, as well as whether voters actually are manipulated in some fashion by their exposure to advertising. We are hopeful that the analysis in this book will go a long way in helping citizens, pundits, and political operatives more accurately assess the role television ads play in contemporary American elections.

Book Preview

We have merely introduced the story in this chapter, of course. Do ads persuade? If so, when and for which types of voters? Chapter 2 reviews existing literature on political persuasion. We then lay out expectations about the conditions under which ads should matter the most and least. Chapter 3 describes our approach to detecting ad persuasion, which involves matching survey respondents with data on the specific ads, and their characteristics, that were aired in their media markets. Our approach allows us to create a relative, individual-level measure of ad exposure.

Chapter 4 is the first of our empirical chapters to test the expectations derived from our theoretical framework. We explore how the campaign context influences the effectiveness of advertising. Theoretically, the impact of advertising should be different for incumbents, about whom voters know a lot, and their challengers, about whom voters know very little. It should also differ depending on the stage of the campaign (is it early, when people know little about the candidate, or later on?), and the competitiveness of the race. We explore these ideas using data from the U.S. Senate campaigns from 2000 and 2004 and the presidential general elections of 2000 and 2004. Certainly, it would be nice to be able to look at even more races, such as Senate primaries, House primaries, and House general elections. We suspect that ad campaigns in these races influence citizens considerably, given that voters have relatively little information about such candidates, especially challengers. The survey data, however, are too scant—and levels of advertising are generally too low—to be able to analyze these races using our approach.

Chapter 5 explores how the characteristics of the advertisements to which viewers are exposed have an impact on advertising's effectiveness. We develop different accounts of how an ad's characteristics should influence its effectiveness: one that is tone-based (i.e., whether the ads are negative or positive) and one that is emotion-based, focusing specifically on whether the ads make appeals to fear, anger, or enthusiasm.

Chapter 6 shifts from how the characteristics of the ads matter to how the characteristics of the viewer might influence an ad's effectiveness. We focus on two specific viewer characteristics: partisanship and political knowledge. Theory suggests that political independents should be most influenced by advertising, all else being equal, because they lack a partisan anchor, whereas partisans may be "brought home" by messages from candidate of their own party, as well. We also suggest that it is those with low political knowledge who should be most influenced by advertising, because those high in knowledge are able to resist messages contrary to their own political predispositions.

Chapter 7 investigates how televised political advertising can have an influence on viewers who are exposed to such ads in the news media or on the Internet. We demonstrate that there has been substantial discussion of political advertising by the news media in recent elections and that such discussion has increased over the most recent election cycles. One focus of the chapter is an examination of advertising exposure in 2006, and we split exposure into two types: exposure to thirty-second commercials themselves and exposure to news coverage of advertising, both in newspapers and on local television news broadcasts. We look for evidence that exposure to media coverage of ads, as opposed to exposure during commercial breaks, has any influence on vote choice. We also spend considerable time discussing the development of online tools that enhance the possibilities to persuade voters.

In the final chapter, we offer suggestions for the study of advertising in the future, and we consider key normative questions related to the influence of political advertising. For example, given the evidence in the book, are political ads a vital component of American democracy, giving people the information they need to align their voting choice with their political predispositions? Or are political ads manipulators, leading people to cast ballots in ways they might not normally? Political advertising has been ubiquitous in all recent election cycles, and it is likely to remain so for many years. This book contributes an important body of evidence that addresses what ads persuade, when they persuade, and whom they persuade. In doing so, the book speaks to claims that advertising has a deleterious effect on American democracy.

2 > The Problem of Persuasion

OUR QUESTION in this book is simply put: Is political advertising little more than background noise, or do ads influence the choices that voters make? There are two ways by which advertising could influence a person's vote choice—or, at least, who wins an election. The first possibility, and the most direct, is that advertising may influence people's evaluations of political candidates. As advertising makes one candidate look more or less attractive, the likelihood that the viewer will cast a vote for that candidate will rise or decline. The second possibility is a bit more indirect—namely, advertising may encourage or discourage supporters of one candidate from turning out to vote on Election Day. Thus, a candidate may win an election not because she has more supporters among the electorate but because her supporters are more fired up about going to the polls.

Our focus in this book is on the first way in which advertising might affect outcomes: by directly affecting people's evaluations of candidates. Why do we focus on this route of influence? One reason is that the impact of advertising, especially negative advertising, on voter turnout has already been studied extensively. For much of the 1990s, scholars were motivated to study the relationship between ad tone and voter turnout because of the controversial claim of Ansolabehere and Iyengar (1995) that negative ads demobilized citizens and depressed election turnout. Much ink has already been spilled on this question, and we have waded into the debate ourselves as recently as 2008 (Franz, Freedman, Goldstein, and Ridout 2008). Indeed, we would suggest that scholars have devoted more time to investigating important *byproduct* effects of advertising, such as the relationship between advertising tone and citizens' involvement or participation in the political system (Ansolabehere and Iyengar 1995; Djupe and Peterson 2002; Goldstein and Freedman 1999; Kahn and Kenney 1999; Lau and Pomper 2004; Martin 2004; Peterson and Djupe 2005) than they have to studying ad persuasion.[1]

The other reason we focus on the more direct impacts of advertising on candidate evaluations and voting choice is that most recent evidence suggests that advertising's impact on voter turnout is likely very small, if it exists at all (Jackson, Mondak, and Huckfeldt 2009; Krasno and Green 2008; Lau, Sigelman, and Rovner 2007). In short, while the debate over ad tone and turnout seems to have reached some consensus, there still seems to be much to learn about the extent of advertising's direct impact on voting choice.

To be fair, the most recent and most sophisticated experimental and observational studies in this area do find that advertising is effective in moving votes.[2] For instance, one study found that the difference in the volume of state-level presidential advertising between the two major-party candidates predicted vote choice in both 2000 and 2004 (Shaw 2006); an increase of 1,000 gross ratings points from a candidate was worth about 0.1 percent of the vote. In addition, studies based on survey evidence (Goldstein and Freedman 2000; Huber and Arceneaux 2007) have also concluded that advertising does move voters. Yet even with a renewed focus on such questions, an important

---

[1] As we have asserted elsewhere (Franz, Freedman, Goldstein, and Ridout 2007), such questions *are* vitally important for American democracy, but they are of less interest to candidates and campaign decision makers, who share a single, simple objective: winning elections. As such, we label them byproduct effects, but we recognize that they are direct effects and worthy of study in their own right.

[2] A number of studies have asked about the relationship between ads and voter persuasion, but many of these studies are fairly limited in that they focus on one contest or use predominately a handful of undergraduates in experimental settings. We discuss these studies in our literature review in this chapter, but we also devote Chapter 3 to a more specific discussion of research design challenges.

question remains: under what conditions is advertising most likely to matter for voting choice?

We argue that the impact of political advertising in a political campaign is likely contingent and depends on three factors: the campaign context in which ads are aired; the characteristics of the ads; and the receiver of the ad messages. In the sections that follow, we review the existing literature on these claims and offer a series of testable hypotheses that we explore in Chapters 4–6.

Persuasion and the Campaign Environment

One of the central factors that is likely to influence the effectiveness of political advertising is the context of the race or the campaign environment. The campaign environment, to us, refers to a variety of things: the office at stake (president, U.S. senator, or county coroner), the stage of the campaign (months before the election or the week before Election Day), the status of the candidate (incumbent, challenger, or candidate in an open-seat race), and the competitiveness of the race. There are good reasons to expect that all of these factors related to the campaign environment will moderate the effectiveness of the ad campaign.

For example, during the presidential general election, the vast majority of voters are aware of the candidates and already have opinions of them, perhaps making it much more difficult for advertising to have a persuasive impact. As of late July 2008, for instance, only 7 percent of respondents in a CBS News poll said they did not know enough about John McCain to have an opinion of him; the comparable figure for Barack Obama was 5 percent.[3] In contrast, U.S. Senate candidates vary considerably in how well known they are to the electorate (Jacobson 2008), but they are almost always less well known than general election presidential candidates. This may open the door for advertising to make an impact. As such, our initial expectation for the types of races we examine is that ads will have a greater impact in

---

[3] The data are from a CBS News poll, fielded July 31–August 5, 2008. The sample was composed of 906 adults nationwide. The results are available online at http://www.polling report.com/people.htm (accessed August 8, 2008).

Senate general election races than in the presidential general election. Moreover, given that the voters exit the presidential nomination season with more knowledge about the presidential candidates than they had before entering it, we expect advertising to matter more in the nomination season than during the general election season.

Incumbency status in the race is another important aspect of the race environment that should influence the effectiveness of political advertising at moving votes. Incumbents generally enter a race well known by the electorate and are almost always better known than those candidates who are challenging them (Jacobson 2008). Thus, voters' images of incumbents are generally quite solid, based on a lot of information, making it more difficult for incumbents to move voters through their advertising. By contrast, challengers' advertising should have a greater opportunity to shape the image of the sponsoring candidate (all else being equal)—and, in consequence, influence support for the challenger.

One study that examines the differential effectiveness of incumbent and challenger advertising in the context of several U.S. Senate races from 1996, however, fails to find much difference in their effectiveness (Goldstein and Freedman 2000). Despite finding strong advertising effects in Senate races that year, the estimated effects of incumbent and challenger ad exposure in a model predicting voting choice were opposite in direction but almost identical in magnitude. This suggests that the size of the impact of incumbents' and challengers' advertising is essentially the same. Of course, this finding stands in contrast to our expectation that advertising will be more effective for challengers.

What about open-seat races? We expect that advertising by candidates in open-seat races, which generally feature two less-well-known candidates because neither is an incumbent, to have a greater impact than advertising by incumbents. The reasoning for this is straightforward. Open Senate seats represent the best chance for a party to steal a seat from the other party; thus, candidates in such races almost always have access to the substantial monetary resources necessary to buy ads. This also creates a lot of interest among the public. Moreover, candidates in these races, while perhaps fairly prominent in a state, are generally not as well known as the incumbents who are stepping down. Thus, advertising is likely to make a difference given relatively unknown candidates, an intense advertising campaign, and a high degree of public interest.

The timing of the advertising also deserves some discussion. Here we have competing expectations. On the one hand, ads aired early during a campaign should have more potential to influence support for a candidate, given that less is known about the candidates early on. In general, this follows from what might be considered a truism: early information is simply more valuable. On the other hand, early ads are aired at a time in which many voters often are not paying close attention to the race. If early ads are being ignored, then their potential to move the vote may be minimal. Ultimately, we find more value in the former expectation. Because campaigns are so often concerned with setting the agenda and getting out in front of competitors, we believe that the evidence should reveal effects at their strongest when ads are aired earlier in the campaign.[4]

Finally, competitiveness is another aspect of the campaign environment that may have an influence on the impact of advertising. In general, we believe that the more competitive the race, the more impact advertising should have. Why? Voters tend to pay more attention to the campaign in more competitive races, and there is more advertising in such campaigns. On the other hand, of course, more competitive races feature more balanced flows of messages from competing candidates. Ads from one candidate generally do not vastly outnumber those from the other in a competitive race. Thus, it is unlikely that a voter will receive, say, four times as many messages from one candidate as from his or her opponent. Furthermore, there are many other sources of information for the voter in an intense campaign and, thus, other potential persuasive messages out there competing for the voter's attention.

---

[4] As we will discuss in Chapter 3, we build this expectation directly into our measurement of advertising exposure. When we estimate the volume of survey respondents' ad exposure, we take the natural log of the estimate. This implies an expectation on our part that the first set of ads viewed by a voter will have more impact than the last set of ads. With the discussion in this chapter, however, we actually mean something simpler: ads on the air earlier in the campaign (spring or summer of the election year) will have more impact than ads aired in late September or October.

Ultimately, this discussion establishes our first major set of expectations, which we term the context hypothesis. On balance, the context hypothesis expects:

- Senate general election ads to have a greater effect than presidential general election ads
- Presidential nomination-race ads to have a greater effect than presidential general election ads
- Challengers' ads to have a greater effect than incumbents' ads
- Open-seat ads to have a greater effect than ads in races featuring an incumbent

In our last two expectations, we recognize that the alternative hypotheses are also quite compelling.

- We predict that early ads will have a greater influence than later ads, though late ads potentially will have more impact because the election is drawing close and the stakes are higher.
- Ads in competitive races should have a greater impact than ads in non-competitive races, though such contexts may also feature competing information that might attenuate advertising's effect.

Persuasion and Ad Characteristics

Although the campaign environment surely helps moderate the influence of political advertising, the characteristics of the ads themselves are likely to matter, as well. For example, scholars have identified many possibilities for how advertising tone—and specifically, negativity—might influence voting choice. Two are central to such discussions. The first is what we label an intended effects model, in which negative advertising should lower the evaluations of the attacked candidate, leading to greater support for the sponsor of the ad.

Political consultants are convinced that negative ads work in this way. The Republican strategist Roger Stone suggests, "People like a fight. Put up an ad about the intricacies of the federal budget, and people will turn the channel. Put up an ad like the Swift boat one, that creates an indelible image in the voter's mind" (Rutenberg and Zernike 2004). Steve McMahon, a Democratic political strategist, agrees: "Focus groups will tell you they hate negative ads and love positive ads. But call them back four days later and the only thing they can remember are the negative ones" (Rutenberg and Zernike 2004).

Surprisingly, there is very little evidence to demonstrate that negative advertising consistently has its intended impact. One study that speaks to the relationship between tone and voting choice is Lau and Pomper's (2004) book-length examination of negative campaigning in Senate elections. They spend two chapters investigating tone's impact on votes received. Instead of looking specifically at the tone of advertising, however, they examined the tone of the campaign, as measured by a content analysis of newspapers. Their general conclusion was that negative campaigning can help reduce votes for the attacked candidate, but typically only for a challenger who is attacking an incumbent.

Fridkin and Kenney (2004) also found intended effects in the 1988–1992 U.S. Senate elections, but only with certain types of negative messages. Only negative messages deemed to be legitimate—those discussing issues considered relevant to a campaign discussion—lowered evaluations of the targeted candidate. "Mudslinging" campaigns did not work as intended. Although insightful, their work focused on the impact of such messages on candidate evaluations; they did not examine voting choice, although presumably candidate evaluations and voting choice are linked. A number of experimental studies, including Pinkleton (1997) and Kaid (1997), also support the intended effects hypothesis.

A second possible effect of negative advertising is backlash (Garramone 1984; Lemert, Wanta, and Lee 1999). That is, viewers of negative advertising might lower their evaluations of the sponsoring candidates if they believe the advertising is untruthful or unfair and thus would be more likely to vote against that candidate. In a sense, then, viewers would be punishing candidates for going negative. There is suggestive evidence in the literature that such a backlash is not infrequent. More specifically, Lau, Sigelman, and Rovner (2007) performed a meta-analysis of the large literature on campaign tone and persuasion. They note that in all of the studies they examined, there were forty reported effects on the impact of negativity; backlash effects of varying sizes were noted in thirty-three of them.[5]

On balance, then, the risk of a backlash is real, and political consultants and candidates are very sensitive to the possibility. With any message that attacks the opposition comes the possibility that viewers will reject instead the messenger. What remains a mystery in these models linking ad tone and vote choice, however, is the specific mechanism that connects the two, which is generally not well specified. One possible mechanism is provided by a cognitive account. In a cognitive account, people presumably learn positive information about the ad's sponsor or negative information about the ad's target and that leads them to update their evaluations of the candidates. Another possibility is provided by an affect transfer account. In this account, a promotional ad presumably generates positive feelings toward the sponsor, and a negative ad generates negative feelings toward the target. In truth, though, most research examining the link between tone and voting choice seems to be agnostic about whether the mechanism is primarily an informational one or an emotionally based one in which the affect in the ad is transferred to the featured candidate.

Recently, however, scholars have begun to move beyond valence models that rely on a simple positive–negative conception of tone. One simple modification is to consider also contrast ads (Jamieson, Waldman, and Sherr 2000), where ads that compare candidates (their issue positions or their personal characteristics) are treated differently from ads strictly attacking the opposition—perhaps mitigating the possibility of a backlash. In our own research, we have often collapsed negative and contrast ads into one category (Franz, Freedman, Gold-

---

[5] A third possible effect of negative advertising is that it lowers evaluations of both candidates, which is called the double-impairment effect (Basil, Schooler, and Reeves 1991; Merritt 1984; Shapiro and Rieger 1992). Here, the ad has its intended effect—it lowers evaluations of the attacked candidate—and it has a backlash. Fridkin and Kenney (2004) found this double-impairment effect for certain types of negative campaigns—those described as "mudslinging." Others have described a victim syndrome effect in which viewers feel sorry for attacked candidates and thus increase their evaluations of them. For instance, viewers of Progressive–Conservative party ads in Canada from 1993 evaluated the Liberal Party leader Jean Chrétien more positively after seeing ads that highlighted his facial paralysis (Haddock and Zanna 1993).

stein, and Ridout 2007; Ridout and Franz 2008) because the latter ads by definition contain attacks on the opposing candidate. Such an approach might conceivably be masking real differences in the nature of these ads, however. Brooks and Geer (2007, 3) note this challenge: "When studying effects of campaign tone, we need to incorporate a more nuanced view of campaign negativity than is typically assumed by scholars." They do this in their study of political engagement by considering the (in)civility of campaign discourse (see also Fridkin and Kenney 2008; Sigelman and Park 2007).

Another approach focuses on the specific, discrete emotions (e.g., anger, compassion, pride) elicited by advertising, which allows for a more nuanced treatment of different ad types. In one conception, this account is equivalent to the affect transfer model mentioned above in that ads that elicit anger, fear, or anxiety transfer those negative emotions to the targeted candidate, resulting in lower voter evaluations of that candidate and a lower likelihood of voting for that candidate. More simply, advertising might potentially scare or anger viewers into voting for certain candidates. Likewise, emotions such as pride and enthusiasm are transferred to the ad's sponsor, leading to higher voter evaluations of the candidate and a greater likelihood of voting for that sponsor.

There have, however, been some challenges to the affect transfer explanation (Brader 2006). The first objection is that all emotions— even if they are of the same valence (i.e., all positive or all negative)— do not necessarily have the same effects on political thinking and behavior. For instance, some research has posited that while anxiety elicited by a fear appeal leads to avoidance behavior and heightened vigilance, this is not the case for anger, which is associated with less thorough cognitive processing (Huddy, Feldman, and Cassese 2007). On this last point, it may be the case that an angry message induces an emotional wall that limits its persuasive impact. A second problem with the affect transfer explanation is that, increasingly, empirical research has failed to support it. For instance, Brader's (2006) experimental research found that exposure to enthusiasm cues embedded in political ads reduced affect toward the ad's sponsor instead of making receivers feel more warmly toward the candidate.

Others have offered alternatives to the affect transfer account, including the theory of affective intelligence (Marcus, Neuman, and MacKuen 2000). This theory posits that humans have two affective subsystems: the disposition system and the surveillance system. The emotions of the disposition system (generally thought of as enthusiasm) provide citizens with feedback on the activities they pursue. As humans learn through the repeated guidance of the disposition system, they develop habits: "We sustain those habits about which we feel enthusiastic and we abandon those that cause us despair" (Marcus, Neuman, and MacKuen 2000, 10). In the realm of politics, one can think of many situations in which voters rely on habit and predisposition, such as in casting ballots.

Brader (2006) has translated the ideas of the affective intelligence into expectations about exposure to various types of emotional appeals in political advertising. For example, if the affective intelligence model is correct, appeals to enthusiasm should strengthen support for the sponsoring candidate *among supporters* (who use enthusiasm cues to reinforce predispositions) but should have no influence on the support of initial opponents (who have no existing predisposition toward the candidate that enthusiasm appeals can reinforce). In this sense, enthusiasm cues should increase the role of habit and prior preferences.

We are unable to assert at this point which of these many models of how the characteristics of ads influence vote choice is "correct" or which one is better than the others. But we do test these competing models in Chapter 5, pitting the intended effects and backlash effects models against each other in two separate characterizations of political ads: positive–negative-contrast ads and ads featuring fear, anger, and enthusiasm. In other words, we ask: are negative ads or ads that appeal to fear and anger most likely to help or hinder the sponsor?

We also investigate two other hypotheses implicit in this discussion. First, we test a discrete emotions model that expects fear ad exposure (which should stimulate political action) and anger ad exposure (which is expected to shut down voter processing) to have different effects. We also test for the moderating role of initial support in the effectiveness of enthusiasm appeals.

Persuasion and Receiver Characteristics

Although the context of the race and the characteristics of the ads themselves all should influence the effectiveness of an ad campaign, one should not overlook how the characteristics of those who receive the ads play a role. There are two receiver characteristics that we believe to be the most important moderators of ad effectiveness: the receiver's level of political awareness and his or her partisanship.

The moderating influence of political awareness on persuasion is expressed most clearly and most succinctly in the existing scholarship through the dosage-resistance model (Iyengar and Simon 2000; Krosnick and Brannon 1993). The basics of the model are explained as follows. Every voter is aligned at some point on the political awareness scale. Awareness is Zaller's (1992) preferred term for this concept, although we will use the terms "political information," "political sophistication," and "political knowledge" interchangeably, as well. At the low end are political novices who know little about politics. When asked, for example, to identify the majority party in Congress or the job that Nicolas Sarkozy holds, they cannot. They may very well be interested in politics or care about the larger issues, but in practical terms they have no pre-existing store of political information. This is in contrast to the political junkies on the high end of the scale who know everything there is to know about politics and keep tabs on political events in ways similar to the millions of Americans who track fantasy baseball scores.

These varying levels of political awareness are expected to moderate to a great degree the impact of political information that floods American voters during an election season. The model first predicts that as political awareness rises, the greater the chance voters will "receive" the message—in other words, the greater the chance they will understand and take in political events or news. As an example, imagine a voter watching television who is exposed to a candidate's ad about health care. The message is "received" if the voter understands the point of the ad and is able to discuss the points and arguments raised in the message. Zaller (1992) calls the assumed relationship between reception and political awareness his "reception axiom."

However, with rising political awareness comes a decline in the "yielding" potential of each voter. Yielding in this sense could be understood as the probability that a voter is persuadable. For voters with no political knowledge, new information might easily sway any decision making. But for voters with large stores of political information, new messages are harder to break through and more easily argued against.

When we combine "reception" and "yielding," we can see that those on the low end of the awareness scale need the information the most (high yielding potential) but are less likely to understand it (low reception potential). Those on the high end of the scale are more likely to understand it (high chance of reception) but are less likely to need it (low yielding potential). The model consequently predicts that, in many situations, those with moderate levels of political information are most likely to "accept" a political message.

However, whether the peak of influence is near the top or the bottom of the sophistication scale will depend on a couple of key factors. First, it depends on the intensity of the information environment. The more messages that are being sent, the more likely that people with lower levels of political awareness will receive those messages. Even those low in political knowledge can receive political information when the message environment is particularly intense (Zaller 1992, 267). Indeed, there is some evidence that in presidential elections, low-information voters are the group that is most responsive to national conditions when deciding for whom to vote (Zaller 2004). Thus, the peak of influence may be toward the low end of the political awareness scale when the campaign environment is intense and toward the high end of the political awareness scale when there are few messages being sent.

Because presidential campaigns certainly qualify as intense campaign environments, we can reasonably expect that advertising for Al Gore, George Bush, or John Kerry might prove powerful even among those who are low in political awareness. But will this be the case, as well, in U.S. Senate races, which vary considerably in intensity, but—at least, on average—feature less political advertising? We expect the answer to be yes, and the reason has to do with the nature of political advertising.

The ease with which a political message can be understood is the other factor that may determine whether maximum influence is found among those with lower or higher levels of political awareness. This is especially important when speaking of political advertising. Because thirty-second spots typically are expertly designed to convey a simple message and often to appeal to emotions, it is likely that low-information voters will be able to take in, and be affected by, political ads. This stands in contrast to political messages that are more difficult to understand. For example, hour-long discussions on Sunday morning talk shows; interviews with candidates or reports on *60 Minutes* or *Nightline*; exposés in *Vanity Fair* or *Newsweek*; policy statements on candidates' websites or blogs—these all require a considerable investment by the receiver of the message and can often be too complicated for many citizens to take in.

Television ads, by contrast, are designed to convey a simple, evocative message in short bursts. Even knowing nothing about the issues or the candidates does not preclude one from reacting to a compelling message about family, morals, the economy, or national security. In fact, a common criticism of television ads is that they dumb down American politics into something akin to selling toothpaste (Greenfield and Bruno 1972). Thus, we expect political advertising to have its greatest influence on low-information citizens, especially when advertising is intense. This is because—with an intense ad environment—novices have a high chance of reception *and* a high yielding potential. We term this our knowledge hypothesis.

A few studies have examined the influence of political advertising on people with varying levels of political knowledge. Valentino, Hutchings, and Williams (2004), for example, use an experimental design and find persuasion effects most commonly among low-information voters, which is in line with our expectations. Some of our earlier work (Franz, Freedman, Goldstein, and Ridout 2007) reaches the same conclusion. We found that political advertising had as much of an impact on the knowledge and political interest of low-information citizens as on the knowledge and interest of high-information citizens, suggesting that even those without much political awareness are able to receive the messages of television ads.[6] Huber and Arceneaux (2007), however,

---

[6] There is some evidence in this earlier work of ours that political novices are even more responsive in terms of knowledge and interest. Those on the low end of political awareness have more to gain; therefore, these gains tend to be higher in relative terms.

use the 2000 Annenberg panel survey to find evidence that the moderately informed are most influenced by political advertising.

Some research even concludes that political messages have the most impact on the *most highly* aware citizens. Most of these findings, however, deal not with political advertising but with *news messages* more generally. Moreover, most of these studies are concerned with priming (i.e., the activation of issues that voters use to evaluate candidates), not persuasion (Druckman 2004; Krosnick and Brannon 1993; Miller and Krosnick 2000). On that score, Krosnick and Brannon (1993, 972) argue that those high in knowledge "have a greater ability to interpret, encode, store, and retrieve new information." We find this argument, as we have mentioned, most compelling for situations in which the information environment is low intensity and for news reports that are more difficult to understand, not for political ads.

The second characteristic of the receiver that should moderate the effectiveness of political advertising is the individual's partisanship. Our partisan hypothesis is rooted less in revising existing theory than it is testing some basic predictions. Indeed, of the scholarship on the moderating effects of political ads, partisanship is the dominant focus. We expect that political independents, because they are unlikely to resist the messages of any candidate as being inconsistent with their existing beliefs, will be influenced by exposure to advertising from both candidates. In contrast, Democratic advertising will have little impact on Republicans, but it *will* increase support for the sponsor among Democrats. The same story applies to Republicans' advertising, which is likely to have its greatest impact on political independents and Republicans. Thus, one overall effect of the campaign—in addition to influencing independents—is to bring partisans home, just as Lazarsfeld, Berelson, and Gaudet (1944) noted more than a half-century ago.

The literature that speaks to this hypothesis has offered a mixed assessment of its validity. Chang (2003) reported that it was partisans who were influenced most by ad exposure, not political independents. Moreover, the series of experiments by Ansolabehere and Iyengar (1995, 77) supported the claim that nonpartisan voters are "the least receptive to political advertising." Instead, they reported that the effect of advertising is mainly reinforcement, moving voters to cast ballots in line with their partisan inclinations. But a different experimental study (Kaid 1997) found some evidence for the opposite conclusion: that political independents were more influenced by watching a political spot than were partisans. Pfau, Holbert, Szabo, and Kaminski (2002) went further, finding differences between partisans and unaffiliated subjects depending on ad sponsor and type; candidate contrast ads appeared to have the strongest effect on Republicans, while candidates' positive ads and interest group ads had the strongest effect on independents.[7]

Conclusion

This chapter has outlined our expectations for how the impact of political advertising varies depending on the campaign environment, the characteristics of the ads themselves, and the characteristics of the ad receiver. We should be clear here, however, about the nature of our contribution to the existing research. In offering predictions about the moderating influence of the campaign environment, for example, we borrow heavily from others' research. While there is little scholarship specifically comparing ad effects across race contexts, our expectations come directly from what years of scholarship has taught us about when campaigns more generally matter. In offering predictions about the effects of ad characteristics, we have learned a great deal from the very rich and still growing work on ad tone and the rapidly expanding work on emotions in campaigns. To that end, it is time to consider the characteristics of ads in new and unique ways. As to the moderating effect of receiver characteristics, especially as they relate to the dosage-resistance model, we believe it is important to consider not only the intensity of the message but also the nature of the message. Some messages are received by those low in political sophistication because those messages are repeated time and time again (as in presidential campaigns), but other messages are received by those low in political sophistication because the message itself is easy to understand (as with thirty-second ads in all types of campaigns).

---

[7] Other research examining the impact of campaign events—not political advertising specifically—also concluded that political independents were the most influenced (Hillygus and Jackman 2003).

One limitation of our study is that it is primarily a study of *televised* political ads, not a study of campaign communications more generally. We will say very little, for example, about the persuasive appeal of radio ads (of which there is very little scholarly work; see Geer and Geer 2003), billboard advertisements and lawn signs (of which we can locate no major studies; however, see Addonizio, Green, and Glaser 2007), or direct mail and peer-to-peer contacts (see Hillygus and Shields 2009). The conclusions that we draw about the persuasiveness of political ads, then, do not necessarily generalize to other forms of campaign communications. In fact, some suggest that micro-targeted messages conveyed via direct mail might be even more persuasive than political ads (Hillygus and Shields 2009). Such targeted appeals can be tailored to fit the issue needs or interests of specific voters and are subject to less scrutiny by the news media. The idea is that the more personal the message, the more potential it has to persuade. Examining this claim by comparing the relative persuasiveness of campaign ads with other political messages is certainly a worthwhile pursuit but is beyond what we can accomplish here.

In short, when we considered writing this book, we sat down and listed all of the things we knew about when campaign ads should matter most. We hoped to bring the best available data to bear on these questions. So while our primary contribution is not theoretical, and while our focus is limited to television advertisements, the reach of our data and the reach of our empirical investigations are the particular strengths of this book. In short, our analysis extends far beyond the political contexts of the many studies on political ads that precede ours, and we rely on the very best survey and advertising data. We digress briefly in the next chapter to review those data and methods.

3 A Brief Primer on Data and Research Design

IN THIS SHORT CHAPTER, we describe the data used in the analysis for Chapters 4–6. (In Chapter 7, we switch the focus somewhat and leave the discussion of the methodology employed there to that chapter.) One of the key advantages of our approach in this book is methodological. Most existing research in the study of ad effects relies on laboratory experiments, which have been critically important in helping scholars understand the process by which ads might work (see, e.g., Ansolabehere and Iyengar 1995; Chang 2001; Kahn and Geer 1994; Meirick 2002; Pinkleton 1997, 1998; Valentino, Hutchings, and Williams 2004). It is very difficult, however, to make the transition from the laboratory to what happens in the real world of a campaign. Seeing one or two ads in quick succession just is not the same as seeing a multiplicity of ads from various sources over the course of a lengthy political campaign.

To overcome this challenge, we rely on a combination of survey data and real-world ad-tracking data. We can, therefore, test the effects of exposure to multiple ads in multiple contexts (Senate and presidential races; competitive and non-competitive elections; open seats and races with incumbents). We can also look for these relationships at the individual level, which allows voters in the same media market, state, or county to have very different levels of advertising exposure.

In short, we estimate levels of exposure to advertising for each respondent in our survey data, and that level will vary depending on how much television that person reports having watched and how many ads were aired where that person lives. This approach was used originally by Freedman and Goldstein (1999) to study the effect of ad exposure on turnout and has been used by them, and others, quite extensively to study a range of ad effects (Franz, Freedman, Goldstein, and Ridout 2007; Freedman, Franz, and Goldstein 2004; Martin 2004; Ridout and Franz 2007; Stevens 2009).[1]

Given our examination of a wide variety of real-world political races using this detailed measure of ad exposure, we believe our research contributes something important to the investigation of ad persuasion. Consider briefly the body of research on the persuasive force of negative campaigns. According to Lau, Sigelman, and Rovner (2007), as of 2007, sixty-one studies had been identified that investigate the relationship between negative campaigns (all-encompassing, including media and ad negativity) and persuasion. Of these, forty-one have used experiments (twenty-nine of which involved college students as participants). Of the other twenty, thirteen have been published, while seven were papers presented at conferences. Of the thirteen non-experimental published papers, none measured exposure in the way we do here, and only four looked for ad effects in either multiple years or multiple political contexts.[2] Partly because of the data we employ, we believe this book offers the most comprehensive examination of ad persuasion effects to date.

Of course, many scholars prefer to rely on experiments to test the influence of political advertising. The experiment-versus-survey debate is the classic fault line in the tradeoff between securing external validity (the ability to speak beyond the specific data used) and internal validity (the confidence one has in identified causal relationships).

---

[1] Its usage has generated considerable and fruitful debate within the field of political advertising. For a longer discussion of the measure's validity, see Ridout, Shah, Goldstein, and Franz 2004; Stevens 2008. For a more critical assessment, see Huber and Arceneaux 2007.

[2] These were Bartels 2000; Fridkin and Kenney 2004; Kahn and Kenney 2004; Lau and Pomper 2004. The empirical research on ad persuasion more generally (without regard to ad characteristics) is a bit more limited in volume but has the same reliance on experiments or aggregate-level models: see Huber and Arceneaux 2007; Johnston, Hagen, and Jamieson 2004; Shaw 1999, 2006.

We believe it is paramount that questions about *advertising persuasion* have high external validity, however. In plain terms, knowing the influence of ads in actual campaigns—and in multiple contexts—speaks more strongly to the place of advertising in contemporary American elections than testing the marginal impact of a few ads in highly artificial contexts.

We begin by briefly listing the data sources used in the three chapters that follow. We then describe how we estimated ad exposure and describe the model specification used for the data analyses in the chapters to come.

Survey and Advertising Data

The context for our investigation is the presidential races in 2000 and 2004 and sixty Senate races from both years. To assess the effect of advertising in the presidential and Senate general elections in 2000, we use the two-wave American National Election Studies (ANES). The ANES conducted its pre-election wave ($N = 1,807$) beginning in September 2000, then re-interviewed respondents after the election ($N = 1,555$).[3] The survey contains a full battery of questions, ranging from respondents' voting intentions to their evaluations of various candidates.

To assess ad exposure effects in the 2000 presidential primary season, we rely on polling from the National Annenberg Election Survey, which conducted a rolling cross-section (with a panel component) of more than 90,000 voters during the course of the primary and general election campaigns.[4] We use their panel of respondents in Super Tuesday states: people who were interviewed beginning in early January and then again following the March 7 primaries.

Our source of public opinion data for the general election analysis in 2004 is a three-wave panel survey sponsored by the Center for the Study of Politics at the University of Wisconsin, Madison (UW), and the Center for the Study of Elections and Democracy at Brigham

---

[3] The survey is available online at http://www.electionstudies.org (accessed October 27, 2010).

[4] The survey is available online at http://www.annenbergpublicpolicycenter.org (accessed October 27, 2010).

Young University (BYU). This panel study, with waves in June (N = 2,782), September (N = 1,523), and November (N = 1,438), sampled from the U.S. voting-age population, oversampling potential voters in battleground Senate and presidential states.[5]

To measure the advertising environment, we employed ad-tracking data obtained from the Wisconsin Advertising Project.[6] These data report the date, sponsor, and location (media market) of each ad that aired in the largest media markets in the country—the seventy-five largest in 2000 and the one hundred largest in 2004. The project was most active in the 1998, 2000, 2002, 2004, and 2008 election cycles and has limited data available from the 1996 and 2006 election cycles. We examine the impact of exposure to all pro-candidate ads aired in 2000 and 2004. This means that all of our ad exposure measures include interest group, party, candidate, and candidate/party-coordinated advertisements. Thus, when discussing exposure to Democratic ads in the presidential race in 2004, we are referring to all Kerry ads, Democratic Party ads, and pro-Kerry interest group ads (e.g., those ads paid for by MoveOn.org).[7]

In Figure 3.1, we show the level of Senate and presidential advertising in 2000 by week between mid-June and Election Day. The figure also indicates when the ANES pre-general election panel began. Figure 3.2 does the same for 2004, showing the starting point for the September wave of the BYU–UW panel. Both figures show a steady increase in advertising in the few weeks before Election Day, as might be expected.[8] Advertising totals are generally higher in 2004—as we discussed relative to the presidential race in Chapter 1—but we also have data from more media markets in 2004 than in 2000.

---

[5] Survey details are available online at http://csp.polisci.wisc.edu/BYU_UW (accessed October 27, 2010).

[6] Data are available online at http://wiscadproject.wisc.edu/ (accessed October 27, 2010).

[7] There is very limited research that studies the effectiveness of ads by sponsor. We have identified only five studies: Garramone 1985; Groenendyk and Valentino 2002; Magleby 2004; Pfau, Park, Holbert, and Cho 2001; Pfau, Holbert, Szabo, and Kaminski 2002. In combining all pro-candidate ads, we are assuming that sponsorship is irrelevant.

[8] More can be said about strategies in targeting advertising, of course, but we minimize that discussion in this book. In general, however, ads are concentrated in the most highly competitive races and media markets, especially negative ads. For more information on such dynamics, see Franz, Freedman, Goldstein, and Ridout 2007, chap. 5; Kahn and Kenney 2004, chap. 2; Shaw 2006; West 2008.

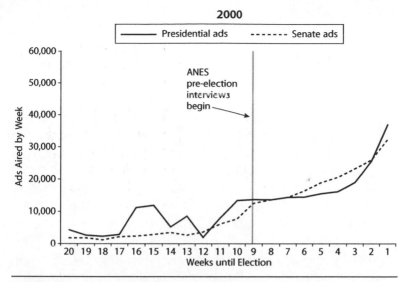

FIGURE 3.1 Ads by week in the 2000 presidential and Senate elections
Source: Wisconsin Advertising Project.
Note: Data are from the top seventy-five media markets.

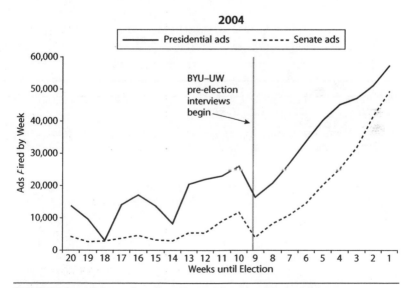

FIGURE 3.2 Ads by week in the 2004 presidential and Senate elections
Source: Wisconsin Advertising Project.
Note: Data are from the top one hundred media markets.

Estimating Advertising Exposure

Using these data, we merged the frequency of different advertising appeals by media market onto the surveys noted above. This allowed us to create an individual-level measure of exposure to political advertising. The calculated measure of exposure takes account of both market-level advertising patterns and individual-level television-viewing habits. The methodology is fairly simple.

First, the ad-tracking data record the television programs during which all political ads aired (top shows in both election years included the local news, *Jeopardy*, *Wheel of Fortune*, morning news shows, and afternoon talk shows). We calculate the number of ads that aired during different shows in each media market. For example, we can determine the total number of Democratic and Republican ads aired in Boston during news, talk shows, and game shows. Second, the surveys asked respondents how often they watched such programs, usually by asking about viewing frequency for a normal week. By appending the ad-frequency data onto each survey—we match each respondent's reported county of residence with the media market that covers that county—we were able to multiply the frequency with which viewers watched each program type by the number of ads aired in the respondent's media market during each program type.

This measure, then, not only takes into account variation across individuals in the amount of television that they view; it also accounts for variation in the volume of advertising across media markets. Thus, a heavy television viewer in a market that does not receive any advertising has low exposure; similarly, a light television viewer in a market inundated with advertising has low exposure.

One assumption of this approach is that each unique ad has an equal impact, and we grant that this assumption may not hold. Some ads may be more effective because of their message or production value; other ads may be more effective because of when they are aired. Given, though, our focus on the overall ad environment of each campaign—an environment in which typically dozens of different ads were aired hundreds of times each over a couple of months—we expect that the influence of particularly effective and ineffective ads will average out.

Indeed, our approach to measuring exposure does not solve all problems; measurement error undoubtedly still exits. For example, are the media consumption questions reliable? That is, do people accurately recall their regular viewership of certain television shows? This is obviously a concern, but consider this: because the surveys ask about regular viewing of thirty- or sixty-minute programs (game shows, local news, morning talk shows), we should have more confidence in these measures than in measures generated from questions about intermittent media recall, such as questions about viewing specific campaign ads. Recall questions are fraught with challenges. Stevens (2008) has shown, for example, that people often overestimate their television watching in survey questions.[9] But our simple questions about regular program viewing should elicit fairly valid responses, given that they concern prolonged and repeated behaviors.

A few additional points are necessary for clarification. First, we can use this setup to estimate both total exposure to Democratic and Republican ads and a specified subset of ads. For example, as we will do in Chapter 5, we estimate exposure to Democratic and Republican negative, contrast, and promotional ads separately, as well as exposure to ads featuring different emotional appeals. This is easily accomplished by aggregating the ad-tracking data by ad content in addition to media market and program type.

Second, the tracking data allow one to estimate exposure up to the date of the survey interview. For post-election surveys, this would include all advertising during the course of the campaign. For pre-election interviews, a more precisely tailored measure is possible. If a respondent was interviewed thirty days before Election Day, for example, the data allow one to construct a measure of exposure that excludes ads broadcast after the date of interview. This is especially important for our analysis of panel data, where we estimate models of exposure to ads aired *between* the survey interviews.

---

[9] The problem of over-reporting is also noted by Prior (2009) in his comparison of Nielsen ratings for network news shows and estimates of those shows' viewing audience derived from self-reports in a large national survey. In short, Prior notes that self-reports overestimate regular viewership of national news by a factor of three (when compared with Nielsen estimates). In contrast, however, a study by the Nielsen-backed Council for Research Excellence, released in March 2009, determined that many people overestimate their use of online media and under-report their consumption of television (Stelter 2009).

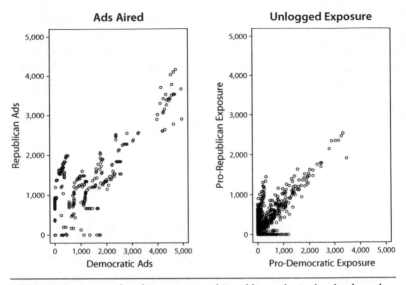

FIGURE 3.3 Scatter plot of Democratic and Republican ads aired and unlogged exposure for the 2004 Senate general election

Note: Entries are for ads aired between respondents' pre- and post-election survey interviews.

To make the estimation process clearer, consider the case of exposure to Senate ads in 2004. In Figure 3.3, we plot the number of pro-Democratic and pro-Republican ads aired in each respondent's (in the BYU–UW panel study) media market between the pre- and post-election interviews. The graph on the left, then, speaks to the ad-information environment of each respondent in the survey. This represents the absolute upper bound of ads that a respondent could have seen. Of course, seeing all of these ads would be impossible unless the respondent was constantly watching television and monitoring all television stations. The panel on the right shows the estimated number of ads seen as scaled *down* by the respondent's viewing habits. We should note that this adjustment for media consumption is likely still an overestimate because viewers often are not paying attention or changing the channel during commercial breaks. Thus, we consider the measure more accurately a *relative* measure of exposure, where those on the high end of the scale are estimated to have seen more ads than those on the low end.

This scaling approach is one of the key advantages to our method of estimating exposure. One problem with these measures, however, is that the Democratic and Republican measures are highly correlated, with the bulk of respondents clustered in the lower left corner, between exposure to zero and one thousand ads. Because of this, statistical models may not have enough leverage to tease out the independent effects of Republican and Democratic advertising.

Fortunately, a simple adjustment can be made that solves this problem (Stevens 2008)—namely, we took the natural log of each measure. This has the pleasing effect of reducing the correlation between exposure to Republican and Democratic advertising. It also penalizes respondents for their tendency to overestimate television viewing. With a logged measure, gross overestimates are not rewarded with consequential rises in estimated exposure. The logging is also informed by theory in that we should never expect the last few ads to have the same effect as the first few. Increasing a viewer's exposure from 100 ads to 200 ads is likely to have more of an impact on his or her voting choice than increasing that viewer's exposure from 2,000 to 2,100 ads. In plain terms, there just is not as much opportunity for an additional ad to change people's opinions when they have already been exposed to hundreds, if not thousands, of ads. This is referred to as "wearout" in the marketing literature (Scott and Solomon 1998).

One might suspect that persuasion effects would be minimized because of the tendency of campaigns to air roughly equal numbers of ads, and thus the ads of competing candidates effectively "cancel out" each other. Although there is some merit to this claim, there are also several instances in our data in which a respondent was exposed to substantially more advertising from one candidate than from that candidate's opponent. Figure 3.4 demonstrates this by plotting each respondent's logged exposure to Republicans' ads against logged exposure to Democrats' ads in the presidential and Senate general elections of 2000 and 2004. For visual ease, while the scales of the x- and y-axes are logged exposure measures—which range from 0 to 8—we show what those numbers mean in terms of the estimated number of ads seen. We also show, with solid gray lines, the locations of each measure's mean value. We add dashed gray lines to indicate one-half standard deviations above and below the mean values. A standard

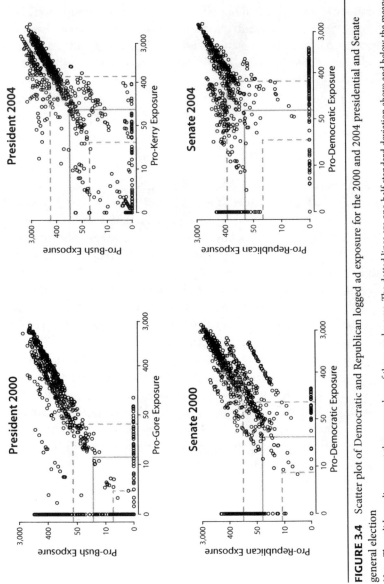

FIGURE 3.4 Scatter plot of Democratic and Republican logged ad exposure for the 2000 and 2004 presidential and Senate general election

Note: The solid gray lines are at the mean values of the *x*- and *y*-axes. The dotted lines are one-half standard deviation above and below the means.

deviation is a common measure of how much spread exists in a group of numbers. Another way to think about this is that about 38 percent of observations fall within one-half standard deviation of the mean if one assumes that those numbers are distributed normally. In future chapters, when demonstrating effects of exposure on the change in support for certain candidates, we will most commonly hold one measure at the mean and vary the other measure by one-half standard deviation about the mean.[10]

Although the observations in all four panels tend to cluster around a 45-degree line, a balanced flow of ad exposure was not always the case. What is more, these imbalances appear to be almost as widespread in the Senate races, depicted in the bottom panels, as in the presidential races, shown on the top. Moreover, there are a number of instances in which respondents are exposed to only one-sided flows of information.

Dependent Variables and Model Specification

To evaluate the various hypotheses we have put forth, we must estimate the impact of ad exposure on reported voting choice and candidate evaluations—our dependent variables. Voting choice is measured as a simple dichotomous variable: vote for Bush or Gore, vote for Bush or Kerry, or vote for the Democratic or Republican U.S. Senate candidate.

Candidate evaluations are operationalized a few different ways, depending on the survey. For example: In the 2000 ANES, respondents were asked whether there was anything in particular that they liked or disliked about the presidential candidates. These were open-ended questions that allowed respondents to list whatever qualities they wished. Each respondent had the opportunity to provide up to five answers. We total likes and dislikes about Gore and Bush, producing four measures (ranging from 0 to 5). In the 2000 ANES, respondents were also asked to report their "feeling-thermometer" scores of Democratic and Republican candidates for the Senate. These range

---

[10] The mean values for exposure in the 2000 Senate and presidential races are lower than in 2004 because the BYU–UW panel in 2004 oversampled in battleground states, thereby including a higher number of respondents who were more likely to live in media markets with some advertising.

from 0 to 100, where 100 represents the most positive evaluation of the candidate. This same measure is used in the Annenberg Super Tuesday study. All other measures of candidate evaluations are "favorability" scores, taken from respondents' reports about whether they strongly or moderately favored or disfavored a certain candidate (or did not know enough to say). This measure is used in the BYU–UW panel survey for presidential and Senate candidates.

Although ad exposure is the central independent variable of concern, all of our models also contained several other important control variables, including respondent demographics (educational attainment, age, gender, race, income, marital status, and region of residence) and respondent attitudes (party identification and level of approval of the president). Years of scholarship have confirmed the importance of these variables in understanding voting choice (see Holbrook 1996, esp. chap. 2).

In addition to these standard controls, we included in the general election presidential models the total number of Gore (2000), Kerry (2004), and Bush (2000, 2004) media market visits in the fall campaign. We added these measures to account for the possibility that the personal appearances of the candidates—and the media coverage that such visits engender—had an independent effect on vote choice. This possibility is particularly important because campaign schedulers and media buyers are likely to target the same states and media markets. Thus, visits by candidates tend to be correlated with ad volume.

In addition to the variables described above, we included a few others in the Senate models. Most important, we included two binary measures indicating whether an incumbent Republican or Democrat was running. As has been well documented, incumbency provides a large—often decisive—advantage in a congressional race (Jacobson 2008).

Full summaries of all variables are listed in Appendix A. We will briefly mention in each empirical chapter the model specifications used for each analysis; in particular, we will note where any specification is unique.

Before proceeding, there are some special statistical considerations in estimating our models of voting choice and candidates' favorability.

As noted, one concern in estimating these models is endogeneity in the relationship between how many ads a candidate runs and that candidate's vote share. More to the point, airing additional advertisements should increase a candidate's share of the vote, but candidates generally air the most advertisements in races in which they face stiff competition, the closest races. This concern in the search for advertising effects is similar to the problem confronting those seeking to estimate the effects of congressional spending on margin of victory (e.g., Green and Krasno 1988, 1990; Jacobson 1990).

To account for this endogeneity, we take advantage of the panel nature of many of the surveys employed here, which allows us to estimate models that include lagged dependent variables. This means that the effect of advertising on a person's vote in the final wave of the panel is conditioned on that person's voting intention in the earlier wave of the panel. By controlling for the dependent variable measured at an earlier time, we attenuate the endogeneity between support for a candidate in an area and the amount of advertising that is aired. In doing so, we go a long way toward increasing the internal validity of our investigations.

Not all surveys have this advantage, however. For example, in the Senate analysis for 2000, we used the ANES, but the pre-election survey did not ask respondents about their intended Senate vote (as it did for the presidential contest). To account for this, we included in our models logged per capita Democratic and Republican spending. Although perhaps not ideal, this does help control for potential endogeneity by including an additional measure of race competitiveness.[11]

There is one final issue that we are unable to address with our statistical models from 2000 and 2004: the possibility that we are neglecting other ways in which people are exposed to political advertising—namely, through print and television news media and through the Internet. We are well aware of this possibility, and we explore it in Chapter 7 with a separate analysis of some U.S. Senate races from 2006.

---

[11] Finally, we estimated all presidential models using robust standard errors. For all Senate models, we clustered on state because there are different candidates with different characteristics in each state and, thus, observations within each state are not completely independent.

Conclusion

Our goal in this chapter was to provide a brief review of our data and research design. We have paid careful attention to developing a quantitative approach that enhances external and internal validity. By using surveys and ad-tracking data, we can speak confidently about the influence of ads on real voters in real political contexts. By estimating a measure of exposure that varies at both the market level and the individual level, we construct the best available measure of ad exposure. By relying mostly on panel data that allows us to control for prior voting intention and candidate evaluations, we maximize the confidence we place in any identified causal relationships.

A significant advantage of our research is the multiple years that we are able to study. Recent studies in the area of ad persuasion have worked hard to enhance both internal validity and the generalizability of findings but have employed research designs different from the one used in this book. For example, Clinton and Owen (2006) use a large-N experimental design with Knowledge Networks data to study persuasion effects in the 2000 presidential election. Huber and Arceneaux (2007) use the National Annenberg Election Survey to examine ad effects in the 2000 presidential general election, looking only at respondents in non-battleground states (under the assumption that endogeneity is of less concern when focusing on citizens incidentally exposed to ads because of proximity to battleground states).[12] We applaud this scholarship, but it has a singular drawback in that each study examines campaigns in a single year and thus is limited in what it can say about race context.

In the next chapter, we begin the empirical story with an analysis of persuasion effects in presidential and Senate races, with the aim of showing how the context of the race matters for the effectiveness of advertising. We begin with an examination of ad persuasion in the presidential general election. We also examine persuasion effects in Senate races that are open, that are competitive, and that feature incumbents, asking whether these larger features of the race environment condition the effectiveness of political advertising.

---

[12] Notably, Krasno and Green (2008) adopt a somewhat similar design for the study of campaign advertising and turnout.

4 ▶ How Race Context Matters

DIFFERENT CAMPAIGNS for office take on vastly different characters. Consider the general election race for president in the year 2000. Al Gore and George W. Bush were neck and neck in the polls for many months, and media coverage of the campaign was extensive, occupying the lead story on television news broadcasts many nights. And advertising, at least in the battleground states, was hard to avoid. If you lived in Albuquerque, for instance, you potentially could have seen 9,132 ads touting one of the presidential candidates on your television screen between July 1 and Election Day. Most Americans knew plenty about the two men vying for the presidency. A CBS News poll taken in mid-July found that only 9 percent of Americans felt they had not heard enough about Gore to have an opinion of him. That number had fallen slightly, to 5 percent, by the week before the election. For Bush, the numbers were similar. Thirteen percent of respondents said in July that they had not heard enough about Bush to have an opinion of him; 5 percent was the comparable figure the week before Election Day. Given that most voters held an opinion of these candidates months before the election—and given the intensity of news coverage of them—one wonders how much room advertising had to shape people's opinions of the candidates.

Contrast this presidential race with the race for U.S. Senate being held in West Virginia the same year. Robert Byrd, the incumbent Democrat, swept to re-election with almost 78 percent of the vote. Byrd had served in the Senate for forty-two years at that time and was probably as well known in West Virginia as the president of the United States. His Republican challenger, David Gallaher, by contrast, was little known before entering the political race—he owned an electrical and general contracting company. Moreover, the news media did little to increase the public's knowledge of him. Our search of the Lexis–Nexis electronic newspaper database was able to locate a single mention of Gallaher between July 1 and Election Day in the *Charleston Daily Mail*, a newspaper based in the state's capital city. The Associated Press in West Virginia mentioned his name just three times during the same four-month period. Gallaher aired not a single political ad in the Charleston–Huntington media market, the only West Virginia media market tracked by the Wisconsin Advertising Project in 2000. Byrd, however, did air an ad touting his history of accomplishments in the state; it aired 420 times. Given how well known Byrd was, however, the money he spent on the ad was likely wasted. Perhaps best capturing the mood of the race was an Associated Press headline a few days before voting commenced: "West Virginia's Senior Senator up for Re-election; Who Knew?"

Now consider a third type of race—one that started out with a challenger who was not all that well known but about whom voters assuredly learned a lot through the course of the campaign. Democrat Debbie Stabenow was a member of the U.S. House of Representatives, one of sixteen serving Michigan, before launching her Senate campaign against the incumbent Republican Spencer Abraham in 2000. The race turned out to be highly competitive, and there was ample opportunity for voters to learn about Stabenow. She was mentioned in eighty-nine articles in the *Detroit News* between July 1 and Election Day, just a few shy of the ninety-eight articles that mentioned Abraham. Moreover, the airwaves were filled with political ads. Abraham and his allies aired an average of just under 4,000 ads in each of Michigan's top media markets between July 1 and Election Day, while Stabenow aired an average of 3,650 ads in those same markets. On November 7, Stabenow defeated Abraham by 1.5 percentage points. It was a race in which advertising likely had a large impact in teaching voters who Debbie Stabenow was and shaping their opinions of her.

These three different campaigns from 2000 point to the wide variety of race contexts that exists. In Chapter 2, we laid out expectations about how the context of the race would influence the effectiveness of political advertising. Let us review them now. The elements of our context hypothesis suggest the following: Senate general election ads should have a greater persuasive effect than presidential general election ads, given that voters generally are less informed about candidates for the U.S. Senate than candidates for the presidency.

With respect to Senate elections, we expect challengers' ads to have a greater effect than incumbents' ads, given that there is generally more to learn about challengers. This should be especially true in more competitive races in which voters are paying more attention. More still, ads aired in open-seat races should have a greater influence on voting choice than ads aired in races featuring an incumbent. This is because such open-seat races generally attract two high-quality candidates and ample media attention. This ensures a rich message environment, but these candidates should still be less well known on average than long-serving incumbent senators.

On these last two points, consider the evidence from the 2004 BYU–UW survey. In the September wave of the poll, only about 8 percent of respondents living in states with incumbent senators felt that they knew too little to express an opinion on their performance in office. Fully half of respondents in these states, however, expressed no knowledge of the challengers in the race. But if we look at only those states with competitive races, the percentage of respondents with no knowledge of the challenger falls to 40 percent. In open-seat races, the percentage of respondents unable to express an opinion about either candidate falls to 30 percent.

In addition to expectations about race context, we predict that the timing of advertising matters. More specifically, we hypothesize that political ads aired early in the campaign will have a greater impact than ads aired later, given voters' relative lack of knowledge about the candidates early on. This does require voters to be paying attention, however, which is questionable, given their propensity to tune out politics until right before Election Day.

Finally, we take one additional approach in this chapter to test the reliability of our survey-based findings. We estimate a series of models using vote totals at the county level, looking for a relationship between market-level ad buys and county election results. The limitation of this approach, of course, is that we cannot use the results to say anything about individual voters. As we noted in Chapter 3, the ability to estimate an individual-level exposure to political advertising requires good survey data (preferably panel surveys) that tap respondents' television viewing habits. Such data are not generally available in most election cycles. By testing for county-level patterns in 2000, 2004 and 2008, however, we can provide some additional evidence that ads matter in the real world—and by how much.

We should also establish outright that our expectations are informed by the available political science scholarship but are certainly open to refutation. Some might suggest, for example, that advertising should matter least in open-seat or competitive elections because of the density of other campaign information, which is expected to drown out or overwhelm advertising. If this alternative is true in the aggregate, we should find very few advertising effects in most contexts, implying a very limited role for political advertising in American politics.

Presidential General Elections of 2000 and 2004

The presidential general election is theoretically the election context in which ads should matter the least. As we noted above, presidential general elections are chock-full of campaign information, and with the ubiquity of Internet access today, interested voters have access to potentially endless news and gossip about the campaign. Of course, such an expectation runs smack into one obvious reality—general election campaigns for president feature hundreds of thousands of ads in dozens of media markets. Campaigns clearly believe that ads make a difference—even in top-of-the-ticket races—as do the two parties and their interest group allies. In fact, the 2000 and 2004 elections featured unprecedented levels of party and interest group independent spending on political commercials (Franz 2008).

To assess whether ads can have an impact in presidential campaigns, we rely on two surveys in the field during the fall election campaigns—the 2000 ANES and the 2004 BYU–UW survey. Both were explained in detail in Chapter 3. And we examine the impact of ad exposure on both vote choice and candidate evaluations.

The general election campaigns of 2000 and 2004 were similar in some ways but also very different. They were similar in that the races featured well-known incumbents—Gore as the incumbent vice-president of 2000 and Bush as incumbent president in 2004—and were very close throughout the fall campaign. But they were also different in that 2000 was a peace and prosperity election while 2004 was a wartime election. One dominant theme of the candidate debates in 2000 was how to spend a Social Security fund *surplus*. But in 2004, candidates were debating the wisdom of going to war in Iraq—and whether and how to get out.

We estimated models predicting voting for Gore as opposed to Bush in 2000 and voting for Kerry as opposed to Bush in 2004. We also estimated models predicting voters' evaluations of each of these presidential candidates. As mentioned in Chapter 3, the measures of candidate evaluation in 2000 come from a series of questions asking voters if they liked or disliked anything in particular about Gore or Bush. These were combined into four composite measures (scaled from 0 stated mentions to a possible 5). Evaluations of Kerry and Bush in 2004 were simpler; respondents were asked to place the candidates on a five-point favorability scale, ranging from very unfavorable to very favorable.

The results of the eight models are listed in Table 4.1. We should say a few words about the setup of this table, which we will mimic for all of our empirical results in this book. Entries are estimated coefficients and z-scores. Coefficients speak to the size of the advertising effect, and z-scores represent the ratio of the coefficient estimate to its standard error. Typically, when a z-score exceeds 1.64, we can have confidence that the statistical relationship between the independent and dependent variable is a true one: nine times out of ten, according to statistical theory, that will be the case. Whether the coefficient and z-score are positive or negative indicates the direction of the relationship. So, for example, if a z-score is −2.34, we can say that as exposure

TABLE 4.1 Effects of Ad Exposure on Vote Choice and Candidate Evaluations in the 2000 and 2004 Presidential General Election

Dependent variable	Gore exposure	Bush exposure
2000 election		
Vote Gore	0.005 (0.03)	0.072 (0.44)
Gore likes	**0.104 (2.62)**	**−0.064 (−1.68)**
Gore dislikes	0.056 (1.59)	−0.017 (−0.5)
Bush likes	0.014 (0.35)	0.024 (0.63)
Bush dislikes	**0.116 (2.92)**	−0.060 (−1.54)

	Kerry exposure	Bush exposure
2004 election		
Vote Kerry	**0.342 (1.96)**	**−0.537 (−2.96)**
Kerry favorability	**0.124 (2.63)**	**−0.135 (−2.65)**
Bush favorability	−0.063 (−1.02)	0.079 (1.21)

Survey: 2000 ANES and 2004 BYU–UW panel study.

Note: Entries are coefficients and z-scores (in parentheses), and each row represents one model. Boldface indicates that the variable is statistically significant at the .10 level. See Appendix B for full-model results. Voting choice models were estimated using logit. Likes and dislikes models were estimated using a generalized linear model, while favorability models were estimated using ordered probit.

to the independent variable *increases,* the dependent variable *decreases,* and this relationship is fairly strong. The bigger the z-score, the more confidence we can have that the relationship is a true one.

Note also that the table excludes the estimates associated with the control variables in the model. This is done to minimize the statistical evidence thrown at the reader. In writing this book, we estimated hundreds of statistical models, including dozens in this chapter alone. Where appropriate, of course, we will discuss the effects of the control measures, but we will keep our focus on the evidence relating to the effects of ad exposure. In Appendix B, however, we list full results for the initial models estimated in this chapter. This should provide ample data for the reader to assess the impacts of relevant control variables. We are not suggesting that these controls are substantively insignificant. To the contrary, as decades of political science scholarship has made clear, "most" of a voter's decision at the ballot box (and evaluations of the candidates) is determined by her partisanship, age, education, income, and other characteristics. Johnston, Hagen, and Jamieson (2004, 38) call this the campaign's "underlying forces."

The table demonstrates that, all else being equal, political ads mattered in both years and in four of the models—for Gore likes and Bush dislikes in 2000 and for Kerry favorability and voting choice in 2004. Consider the influence of ads in the 2000 general election. While ad exposure had no direct impact on voting choice in 2000, its influence on candidate evaluations was noteworthy. An increase in exposure to Gore ads, holding all else constant, raised the number of stated Gore likes; a rise in Bush's exposure, however, lowered the number of reported Gore likes. The substantive impact of advertising in this instance is not small. Moving from a Gore to a Bush ad advantage changes the predicted number of Bush likes by about one-half mention, or 10 percent of the full scale.[1] Increasing exposure to Gore's ads also increased respondents' ability to name qualities they disliked about Governor Bush. Bush's ads were only moderately successful at combating this; the z-score on Bush exposure is marginally insignificant ($z = -1.54$). All told, though, seeing a high quantity of political ads gave voters additional information with which to evaluate the two candidates.

Gore's ads, however, were not without some negative consequence to him. There is at least suggestive evidence that exposure to the vice-president's ads raised his number of dislikes ($z = 1.59$). It of course remains a possibility—especially on the public airwaves—that the pithy thirty-second television spot can work against you. Nearly everyone can cite an example where ever more advertising brings with it a sense of frustration, often directed at the sponsoring candidate. Still, we caution against drawing too deep an inference here. The effect is marginally insignificant and only shows up in this model. (In fact, as we will see in this chapter, there is very little evidence that such an effect is common, at least when measuring exposure to the complete advertising environment). We will devote considerably more time to the possibility of backlash effects in Chapter 5.

Switching to the results of the models for 2004, we see more robust effects in the voting choice model. Exposure to Kerry's ads increased

---

[1] We used the model estimates to create this predicted value, holding all values at their means but varying levels of ad exposure. For a "Gore advantage," we held exposure to Gore's ads at one-half standard deviation above the mean for all respondents and held exposure to Bush's ads at its mean level for all respondents. The reverse was true for a "Bush advantage."

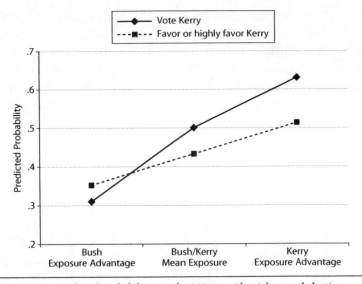

FIGURE 4.1 Predicted probabilities in the 2004 presidential general election

Note: Effects are estimated from results in Table 4.1. Estimates are for a thirty-year-old single woman who identifies as an independent. All other control variables are held at the sample mean.

the likelihood that people would cast their ballots for Kerry, while exposure to Bush's ads increased the chances people would vote for Bush. Kerry's favorability ratings were increased significantly by exposure to his ads and were decreased by exposure to ads sponsored by Bush and his allies. It should come as less of a surprise that the favorability scores for President Bush, who was already well known as the incumbent and who engendered strong opinions—both good and bad—on his presidential performance, were unaffected by either set of ads.

To illustrate the magnitude of the exposure effects in 2004, we estimated a series of predicted probabilities, shown in Figure 4.1. Namely, we show the effect of ad exposure on voting choice and candidate favorability for a hypothetical respondent with slight Kerry and Bush exposure advantages, and for a situation where exposure is at both candidates' mean values. When we speak of an exposure advantage, we mean that exposure to one candidate's advertising is held at one-half standard deviation above the mean across all respondents, while exposure to the other candidate's ads is held at its mean level. More specifically, in the Bush advantage condition, the viewer would be exposed to 600 Bush ads and 120 Kerry ads; In the Kerry advantage condition, the viewer would be exposed to 520 Kerry ads and 140 Bush ads. When exposure to each candidate's ads is held at its mean, our third condition, the viewer is exposed to about 120 Kerry ads and 140 Bush ads. We show these estimates for a thirty-year-old single woman who identifies as an independent.

Under conditions of a Bush exposure advantage of one-half standard deviation (the first condition), the probability of voting for John Kerry is estimated to be 0.30. The probability that this respondent evaluates Kerry favorably is about 0.35. As exposure moves to one of near-parity between the candidates, the Kerry vote probability rises to 0.50, and the likelihood of rating Kerry favorably jumps to 0.43. With a Kerry advantage in exposure, though, the voter now has a more than six in ten chance of voting for him and about a fifty–fifty chance of seeing Kerry in favorable terms.

All told, the results in this section suggest that ads' effects are real. Simply put, our initial expectation of minimal advertising effects in the presidential context was generally disproved. Given such expectations, these results are surprising. We are in good company, however. Other investigations of persuasion in presidential races (ones that use different methodologies from ours) have found effects in 1988, 1992, and 1996 (Shaw 1999), as well as in 2000 (Huber and Arceneaux 2007; Johnston, Hagen, and Jamieson 2004; Shaw 2006) and 2004 (Shaw 2006). Why are we able to find ad effects even in the most unlikely contexts? For one, the assumption that political advertising is unable to compete with other political information may be overblown. That is, political advertising may in fact be the dominant form of campaign information for many voters. Moreover, just because people express an opinion of a candidate in a pre-election poll does not mean that that opinion is beyond influence. Often pollsters will "force" respondents to give opinions even when those opinions are very ill formed or based on little information (Moore 2009). Thus, there is potential, contrary to the frame of our initial discussion, for ads to matter even in high-profile elections.

Presidential Primaries in 2000

Before moving to our investigation of Senate races, we want to examine the impact of advertising in one other context: the battle for the Democratic and Republican presidential nominations in 2000. Presidential primary races are most often multi-candidate affairs, which makes identifying advertising effects even more difficult. This is because advertising from many candidates may be influencing a voter's support for each of the candidates. The contests for the Republican and Democratic nominations in 2000, however, were essentially two-candidate races. Al Gore went head-to-head with Senator Bill Bradley of New Jersey, and Texas Governor George Bush tussled with Arizona Senator John McCain. Moreover, we have good panel survey data with which to test for ad effects—more specifically, the National Annenberg Election Survey (NAES) study of Super Tuesday voters. The NAES initiated pre-election interviews in early January 2000 and concluded on Monday, March 6—one day before elections in sixteen states. The panel included respondents in the twelve states that held both Republican and Democratic contests on March 7 (California, Connecticut, Georgia, Maine, Maryland, Massachusetts, Missouri, New York, Ohio, Rhode Island, Vermont, and Washington).

A bit of history seems in order. Tuesday, March 7, was a clean sweep for Al Gore. He won all of the head-to-head match-ups with Bill Bradley. Still, Bradley was particularly competitive in at least four states, winning 42 percent of the vote in Connecticut, 41 percent in Maine, 41 percent in Rhode Island, and 44 percent in Vermont. He won more than one-third of the vote in Massachusetts, Missouri, and New York.

The Bush–McCain match-up was more competitive. Bush won seven states, and McCain won five. Bush won big in California (60% to McCain's 35%) and Georgia (67% to 28%), and McCain won big in Massachusetts (65% to Bush's 32%), Rhode Island (60% to 36%), and Vermont (61% to 35%). The race was particularly close in Connecticut (49% for McCain and 46% for Bush), Maine (51% for Bush and 44% for McCain), and New York (51% for Bush and 43% for McCain).

To assess the effectiveness of advertising in these states, we estimated models of voting choice and candidate favorability, with individual voters as the unit of analysis. Our empirical setup was identical to the one discussed in the previous section. Our key causal variables are

TABLE 4.2 Effects of Ad Exposure on Voting Choice in 2000 Presidential
Super Tuesday States

Dependent variable	Bush exposure	McCain exposure
Vote Bush	−0.023 (−0.06)	0.073 (0.18)
Bush favorability	0.516 (1.04)	−0.352 (−0.77)
McCain favorability	0.799 (0.81)	−0.869 (−0.88)
	Gore exposure	Bradley exposure
Vote Gore	**0.197 (3.02)**	**−0.192 (−2.17)**
Gore favorability	0.425 (0.76)	−0.712 (−1.17)
Bradley favorability	0.236 (1.60)	−0.023 (−0.11)

Survey: National Annenberg Super Tuesday panel study. Favorability scores are on a 0–100 scale.
Note: Entries are coefficients and z-scores (in parentheses), and each row represents one model. Boldface indicates that the variable is statistically significant at the .10 level. Vote choice models are estimated using logit. Favorability models are estimated using ordinary least squares regression. See
Appendix B for full model results.

exposure to Gore–Bradley and Bush–McCain advertising. To be clear,
these measures account for the estimated volume of ads watched between the pre- and post-election interviews. We also control for respondents' pre-election voting intention (with undecided voters as the base
category), as well as a host of attitudinal and demographic factors.[2]

We should expect advertising to have a significant effect in this
context. Certainly, if ads matter in the general election, they may also
influence voters in this earlier phase of the campaign, when they are
first turning their attention to the presidential election and need information about the major candidates. The results for our six multivariate models (Gore vote, Bush vote, and the favorability scores of the four
major candidates) are reported in Table 4.2.[3] One inference is clear:
ads did not **matter** in the Bush–McCain match-up, as none of the
z-scores exceed 1.64; in fact, only one comes close. They did matter in

[2] As a clarification, the models include two binary measures for initial preference of McCain
or Bush (and, in the Democratic models, initial preference of Bradley or Gore). Because
the Democratic race was a two-person contest, the excluded category is undecided
respondents in the pre-election. Because the Republican contest also featured Steve Forbes
and Alan Keyes (neither of whom performed particularly well in any of the Super Tuesday
states), the excluded category is undecided voters and initial Forbes or Keyes supporters.
[3] The Bush–McCain favorability models include only those respondents who reported a
desire to vote in the Republican primary in the pre-election wave of the survey. The Gore–
Bradley favorability models similarly include only those respondents who reported a
desire to vote in the Democratic primary.

the Gore–Bradley contest, however. Increased exposure to Gore's ads raises the chances of reporting a vote for Gore in the post-election interview, while increased exposure to Bradley's ads decreased the probability of voting for Gore and, in consequence, increased the probability of voting for Bradley.

The strongest determinants of voting choice in the Democratic model, however, were the respondent's pre-election voting intention (hardly a surprise), gender, age, and marital status (see Appendix B). Specifically, older married women moved slightly toward Bradley, while younger unmarried men broke toward Gore.[4] To illustrate how advertising mattered in this race, we show a series of predicted probabilities in Figure 4.2, varying exposure for three types of respondents. Exposure is held at a slight ad exposure advantage for one candidate (defined as one-half standard deviation above the mean) and at the mean value for the other candidate. In concrete terms, a Bradley advantage means that the respondent is expected to have seen about twenty-four pro-Gore ads (3.16 on the logged scale) and about 200 pro-Bradley ads. A Gore advantage assumes average Bradley exposure (about 37 ads) but boosts Gore exposure to one-half standard deviation above its mean, about 125 ads. We show the predicted probability of voting for Gore for a thirty-year-old single man (a type of voter predisposed to favor Gore), a fifty-year-old married woman (a type of voter predisposed to favor Bradley), and an undecided voter.

The figure shows that the thirty-year-old single man has a 0.90 probability of voting for Gore if this voter sees an average number of ads from both Bradley and Gore. As the exposure tips towards one candidate, that probability concurrently shifts, but only moderately (after all, this is a nearly certain Gore voter). By contrast, a fifty-year-old married woman has about a 0.70 probability of voting for Gore on March 7, but a Bradley exposure advantage lowers that probability to about 0.60, certainly making a vote for Bradley a possibility. A Gore advantage, however, nearly guarantees a Gore vote.

---

[4] Keep in mind that these results do not necessarily mean that older, married women as a group favored Bradley or that younger, married men favored Gore writ large. Because we control for pre-election preference, these demographic results mean only that there was a movement away from or toward Gore among these respondents *between* the survey's two waves.

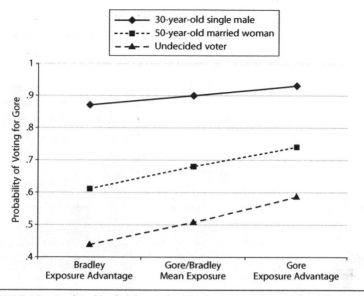

FIGURE 4.2   Predicted probabilities of voting for Gore in the 2000 presidential primaries

Note: Effects are estimated using the results in Table 4.2. All control variables not specified are held at the sample mean.

Finally, a voter who expresses indecision in the pre-election interview (and who has the mean value on all other control measures) has about a fifty–fifty chance of expressing support for Gore in the post-election survey. In this case, ads have a powerful impact. The swing from a Bradley advantage to a Gore advantage moves the predicted probability of voting for Gore from 0.45 to nearly 0.60, a difference of 0.15.

All told, the evidence is compelling that television advertising made some difference in the Democratic nomination battle in 2000. Bradley's ads surely convinced some voters in these Super Tuesday states to cast their ballots for him, but Gore was able to minimize that movement with equally effective spots. Indeed, Gore held a significant advantage in the polls throughout the nomination season, so Bradley's ads may have kept him competitive in certain places and with certain voters.

In fact, Bradley aired more than 3,000 more spots than Gore in the top seventy-five media markets during the entire nominating season

(11,267 for Bradley to Gore's 7,953). In the states where he was most competitive, Bradley held reasonable ad advantages (278 ads in Connecticut to Gore's 178; 210 ads in Maine to Gore's 78; 196 ads in Massachusetts to Gore's 92; 313 ads in Rhode Island to Gore's 52; and 2,441 ads in New York to Gore's 1,236).[5] The individual-level evidence presented in Table 4.2 only reinforces the notion that Bradley's advertising kept him in the hunt, despite the uphill battle he faced against the sitting vice-president.

By contrast, ads did not affect voting choice in the Bush–McCain contest. It is likely that the media coverage of the McCain campaign dwarfed any effects that advertising may have had. McCain's "straight talk express"—a bus tour where he gave unprecedented access to reporters—and his unexpected primary victory in New Hampshire paved the way for dozens of stories, many of them complimentary. Of course, the null findings here do not rule out ad effects in the Republican primary battle. They may have mattered earlier, thereby affecting people's pre-election preferences, or in non-Super Tuesday states.

We cannot say all that much about how these results generalize to other presidential primary campaigns. Certainly, the second half of the Democratic campaign in 2008 largely featured two candidates—Barack Obama and Hillary Clinton—but in most nominating campaigns, the frontloaded calendar usually features multiple candidates vying for their party's nomination. The ad effects in the 2000 primary campaign do, however, support the notion that advertising can play a role at multiple levels of American politics.

Senate General Elections of 2000 and 2004

Indeed, the test for exposure effects in Senate races is an important barometer of this belief. Almost all of the existing studies of ad effects focus on the presidential race, and when the focus does switch to Senate races, the investigation is usually of one or a handful of contests, which limits what we can say generally about ad exposure.[6] Our analysis here examines television ads in sixty Senate races.

---

[5] These numbers are from Ridout 2004, table 1.5.

[6] Some exceptions are Kahn and Kenney (2004) and Lau and Pomper (2004), who examine Senate campaigns in multiple years. These studies, however, investigate the effects of campaign tone generally, not ad tone or advertising more specifically.

TABLE 4.3 Effects of Ad Exposure on Vote Choice and Candidate Evaluations in 2000 and 2004 Senate General Elections

Dependent variable	Democratic exposure	Republican exposure
2000 election		
Vote Democrat	0.062 (0.72)	**−0.143 (−1.69)**
Dem feeling thermometer	0.490 (1.02)	**−0.829 (−1.72)**
Rep feeling thermometer	0.118 (0.16)	0.487 (1.1)
2004 election		
Vote Democrat	**0.223 (1.86)**	**−0.176 (−1.8)**
Dem favorability	0.015 (0.34)	−0.033 (−0.84)
Rep favorability	−0.057 (−1.51)	**0.132 (4.29)**

Survey: 2000 ANES and 2004 BYU–UW panel study.
Note: Entries are coefficients and z-scores (in parentheses), and each row represents one model. Boldface indicates that the variable is statistically significant at the .10 level. See Appendix B for full-model results. Voting choice models are estimated using logit. Favorability models in 2000 are estimated using ordinary least squares regression, while favorability models in 2004 are estimated using ordered probit.

Our data for these tests of Senate ad exposure are the same used in the previous section: the 2000 ANES and the 2004 BYU–UW panel study. We limit the analysis to ads in Senate general election campaigns, however. There is simply too little survey data with appropriate measures to study Senate ads in primary races, although if such tests were employed, we would expect to find widespread evidence of ads' persuasive influence. Later in this chapter, however, we do examine the effects of Senate and presidential general election ads aired in the summer months to test for another implication of our context hypothesis.

Table 4.3 offers a first-cut look at the influence of exposure in Senate races. We make no distinction in this table between the type of race, however, choosing here to pool all respondents in one analysis. Still, we find significant ad effects, and in both years. In the 2000 election, for example, only Republicans' ads mattered, lowering the likelihood of voting for the Democrat and lowering reported feeling-thermometer scores (recall from Chapter 3 that respondents were asked to place candidates on a 0–100 scale, depending on how warmly they felt toward each candidate). In the 2004 election, both Democrats' and Republicans' ads moved respondents' voting choices, and Republicans' ads significantly (and with great statistical confidence; $z = 4.29$) raised respondents' favorability toward GOP candidates.

Exposure to ads from Senate Democrats lowered assessments of Republican candidates, but the statistical estimates here are only suggestive of a relationship.

Our real interest, however, lies in searching for distinctions across different types of Senate races. Looking for such cross-contextual effects, however, requires one extra step in the analysis. In setting up the statistical tests, we multiply the Democratic and Republican exposure measures by indicators for four contexts: open-seat races, competitive races with Democratic incumbents, competitive races with Republican incumbents, and races that are assumed safe.[7] The resulting set of coefficients, then, tells us the effects of ad exposure in these unique circumstances; we can then compare across years, contexts, and party to assess the influence of Senate ads.

To reiterate our hypotheses, we expect exposure to ads in open-seat races to have the greatest effect, followed by ads for those candidates waging a competitive battle against sitting incumbents. We expect the smallest effects for incumbents and for candidates in safe seats.

Results are listed in Table 4.4. The forty-eight coefficient estimates come from six separate models, and we can summarize the results as follows:

- Half of the coefficient estimates for open-seat races are statistically significant. This includes both of the voting choice models in 2000 and 2004, and Democratic favorability scores in 2004.
- For challengers in competitive races (here we are looking at exposure to Democrats' ads in races with Republican incumbents and exposure to Republicans' ads in races with Democratic incumbents), five of twelve estimates are significant.

---

[7] We define competitiveness as any race not listed as safe by *Congressional Quarterly's* fall pre-election assessment. In practical terms, this means even seats that are likely to be won by the Democrat or Republican (those that *Congressional Quarterly* classifies as "leaning" or "favored") are considered competitive. If we restrict the designation of competitive to states listed as "too close to call," we end up with very few incumbent-defended competitive seats, a sad fact of contemporary American elections, notwithstanding the arguments of Brunell (2008), who argues that competitive elections are less than optimal for representative democracy. Ideally for our purposes, this more generous classification stacks the empirical deck against us. This should increase the confidence placed in the identified relationships.

TABLE 4.4 Effects of Ad Exposure on Voting Choice and Candidate Evaluations in 2000 and 2004 Senate General Elections, by Race Type

	Exposure to Democrats' ads				Exposure to Republicans' ads			
	Open seat	Competitive with Dem incumbent	Competitive with Rep incumbent	Safe	Open seat	Competitive with Dem incumbent	Competitive with Rep incumbent	Safe
2000 Senate								
Vote Democrat	**1.07** (**1.85**)	0.114 (0.62)	**0.617** (**2.34**)	−0.014 (−0.17)	**−1.37** (**−2.37**)	−0.157 (−1.13)	**−0.472** (**−1.96**)	−0.145 (−1.25)
Dem feeling thermometer	−7.34 (−1.51)	0.412 (0.59)	**4.83** (**3.14**)	0.357 (0.60)	6.19 (1.26)	−0.487 (−1.06)	**−3.91** (**−2.93**)	−0.587 (−0.67)
Rep feeling thermometer	0.473 (0.12)	0.556 (0.66)	−4.33 (−1.21)	1.14 (1.62)	1.01 (0.26)	0.290 (0.52)	3.28 (1.09)	0.450 (0.51)
2004 Senate								
Vote Democrat	**0.811** (**4.38**)	−0.014 (−0.06)	**0.924** (**3.73**)	0.262 (1.60)	**−0.893** (**−3.70**)	−0.032 (−0.60)	**−0.711** (**−3.56**)	−0.002 (−0.01)
Dem favorability	**0.184** (**2.00**)	0.075 (1.19)	**0.181** (**3.81**)	−0.031 (−0.37)	**−0.137** (**−2.00**)	0.024 (0.74)	−0.044 (−0.56)	−0.040 (−0.76)
Rep favorability	−0.096 (−1.00)	−0.082 (−0.70)	−0.045 (−0.35)	−0.046 (−1.08)	0.095 (0.79)	**0.068** (**2.54**)	0.030 (0.21)	**0.125** (**2.31**)

Survey: 2000 ANES and 2004 BYU-UW panel study.

Note: Entries are coefficients and z-scores (in parentheses), and each row represents one model. Voting choice models are estimated using logit. Favorability models in 2000 are estimated using ordinary least squares regression, while favorability models in 2004 are estimated using ordered probit.

The balance of effects here are for Democratic challengers, who account for four of the five significant relationships, but GOP challengers boosted their own favorability scores with ads in 2004.

♦ For incumbents in competitive races, three of twelve coefficients are statistically significant. All three effects are for Republican incumbents, two in 2000 and one in 2004.

♦ For safe-seat races, one of twelve coefficients is significant. Exposure to Republicans' ads affected favorability toward the Republican candidate in 2004.

Stated simply, Senate ads seem to matter most often in open-seat races and when the sponsor of the race was a challenger in a competitive race. Incumbents receive less of a boost from advertising, which makes sense, given that voters already know so much about these candidates. And candidates in safe races see hardly any return on their investment in television ads.[8]

To demonstrate the impact of ad exposure, we vary ad exposure in four different contexts in 2000 and 2004. These are shown in Table 4.5. Reading down the column, one can see clearly the overwhelming influence of ads in multiple contexts, especially open seats. For example, a young independent voter has a 0.44 probability of voting for the Democratic open-seat candidate in 2000 under average levels of expo-

---

[8] The results showing the impact of ad exposure on Democratic feeling thermometers in 2000 are worth some mention. (The open-seat effects are shown in the second row of Table 4.5.) The effects for open-seat Democratic and Republican exposure are opposite the expected direction (though insignificant), with increased exposure to a candidate's ads lowering his or her favorability. What does this imply? On closer inspection, this strange effect (how could Democrats' and Republicans' ads boost respective vote totals but work in the reverse for feeling-thermometer scores?) is largely the consequence of the open-seat race in New Jersey between the Democrat Jon Corzine and the Republican Bob Franks. The race was controversial in that Corzine, a multimillionaire political novice, spent vast sums of money to win a highly contested primary and then spent even more to pummel Franks in the general election. The race turned particularly negative in the final days of the campaign as both candidates blanketed the airwaves with negative ads. According to the Wisconsin Advertising Project, 7,134 ads were aired in the general election Senate race in New Jersey, just under 60 percent of which contained an attack. As our results highlight, voters who saw a lot of Corzine–Franks ads tended to view the candidates less favorably. If one removes New Jersey from the analysis, though, the feeling-thermometer scores flip in sign, and voting choice effects (already significant) become even stronger.

TABLE 4.5 Predicted Probabilities of Voting for Democratic Candidate in 2000 and 2004 Senate General Elections

	Probability of voting Democrat		
	Rep exposure advantage	Mean exposure	Dem exposure advantage
2000			
All respondents	.44	.49	.53
Open seats	.17	.44	.70
Competitive with Dem incumbent	.64	.68	.71
Competitive with Rep incumbent	.18	.27	.43
2004			
All respondents	.50	.55	.62
Open seats	.26	.51	.68
Competitive with Dem incumbent	.55	.56	.56
Competitive with Rep incumbent	.42	.51	.64

Note: Probabilities are for a thirty-year-old, single white woman who identifies as an independent. She has the mean of all other control variables. Exposure advantage is defined as a one-half standard deviation above the mean. Effects are estimated from results in Tables 4.3 and 4.4.

sure from both candidates. She has a 0.51 probability in 2004. In other words, when the voter is inundated with ads from both sides, the vote is essentially a toss-up. But when a candidate can carve out an ad exposure advantage, the unsure independent voter moves firmly into that candidate's camp. Across the range of exposure in this table (from a Republican advantage to a Democratic one), this voter's probability moves by 0.53 for open-seat races in 2000 (from a 0.17 probability of voting for the Democrat when the respondent sees more Republicans' ads to a 0.70 probability when she sees more Democratic ads) and by 0.42 for an open seat in 2004. Ad exposure here is simply crucial to swaying undecided voters.

Early and Late Ads in 2004

One additional prediction of the context hypothesis is that early ads matter more than ads aired late in the campaign. We argued that this was likely true because candidates are less well known early in the campaign, giving new information a greater chance to have an impact on a voter's view of a candidate. Of course, the alternative is very possible—namely, citizens are paying little attention to Senate and presidential election campaigns in the summer months, preferring to spend quality time at barbeques or on vacation.

Fortunately, we can assess these alternative hypotheses for 2004, because the panel study we use had an initial interview in June. To search for any ad effects, we re-estimated the models for participants interviewed in wave 2 (in the field in September 2004), and conditioned on the respondent's preference in June, using ad exposure between the respondents' two interviews as a key causal variable.[9] We do this for both the Senate and presidential models.

Presidential advertising was quite vigorous in the summer of 2004. There were, on average, about 14,000 ads a week across all of the major markets in the United States. There were significantly fewer ads in most Senate races, although many campaigns were on the air aggressively during July and August.[10] For example, Pete Coors and Ken Salazar in Colorado each aired between fifty and one hundred ads on most days in August. The Democrat Betty Castor of Florida was on the air with high ad volumes for much of August. The same was true of the Democrat Erskine Bowles of North Carolina and his opponent, the Republican Richard Burr. There are numerous other examples in the data, as well. Keep in mind that the traditional wisdom is that Labor Day marks the unofficial starting point of the general election campaign. This may still be true in most Senate campaigns (in spite of the point we made above, Senate candidates had far lower ad buys in

---

[9] There is one wrinkle for the Senate analysis here. Many respondents in the June interviews reported not having enough information to report favorability of the candidates. Thus, when conditioning on Wave 1 preference, these respondents drop out of the analysis. Respondents are unable to express an opinion for many reasons: the primary had not yet determined the nominees, for example, or the candidates had not started airing ads. We attempted a number of alternative specifications to account for this but ultimately decided to omit the first wave's measure of candidate favorability from the Senate favorability model. If we allow the respondents who could not express an opinion to be dropped, the results are consistent with the analysis described in the text, but are slightly weaker. If we preserve the panel structure but include an independent variable for respondents who could not express an opinion, the results are also consistent with what we report. Either way, the general conclusion of this section is unchanged under these alternatives. It should be noted that there is no similar problem in the presidential model; the nominees had been determined by mid-March, and many ads were on the air by June.

[10] We showed the volume of advertising over time in Figures 3.1 and 3.2. The Senate totals in the summer months for those figures include primary election ads. The analysis in this chapter, however, excludes primary ads from the multivariate analysis.

the summer than in the fall) but is certainly no longer true in presidential elections, where the race effectively begins when the major candidates secure their party's nomination (see Franz, Freedman, Goldstein, and Ridout 2007, chap. 5). As such, we have a situation in which presidential advertising was abundant and ongoing, but the volume of Senate advertising varied considerably across races.

The results, which we discuss only here in the text, show a divergence in the effectiveness of early ads. In the presidential race, the ads essentially fell on deaf ears—the average z-score in the voting choice and favorability models is about 0.5. The fall ad campaign, however, was far more effective for Kerry and Bush (see again Table 4.1). In contrast, summer advertising by Senate candidates was generally as effective as fall ad buys. For example, a shift in exposure to advertising by Democrats (again, from one-half standard deviation below the mean to one-half standard deviation above) aired in the summer increased a voter's likelihood of voting for the Democratic candidate by about 0.13; the comparable figure for the fall campaign is 0.14. An increase in exposure to Republicans' ads aired in June, July, and August increased the predicted probability of voting for the Republican by 0.13 and by 0.11 during the fall campaign.

What do these results imply? We can only infer so much from the single-year analysis, but one might posit that the advertising was relatively effective early in Senate races because people knew relatively little about the candidates at that time, and thus this early information may have been quite valuable to voters. People knew quite a bit about the presidential candidates, though, even early in the summer, and citizens may also have been experiencing some lethargy from the presidential primary contest on the Democratic side

County-Level Ad Effects in 2000, 2004, and 2008

The results in this chapter thus far are convincing: ad exposure matters, and it matters largely in the ways that we expected. Overall, television ads can influence voting choice and evaluations of candidates. And they matter in many different contexts. We found ad effects in presidential general elections, presidential nomination races, and U.S.

Senate races, with the strongest effects for open-seat candidates. Where we expected ads to matter least, however—in the presidential general election—they still made a sizable and significant impact. As such, not all of our hypotheses about when ads would influence viewers were borne out.

We are not dispirited by such a refutation, however. In fact, we think of it this way: political advertising is broadly effective in American politics. In some races, where voters are making important choices and less information was previously available about the candidates (such as presidential primaries and open-seat Senate races), advertising can influence ballot-box decisions. But in other cases, even with abundant information available to the voter, advertising can still break through, such as for some incumbent senators and presidential candidates. Spending on advertising, then, is not simply an arms race that amounts to wasted resources in high-profile campaigns. Candidates and their allies in many contexts raise money and air ads for one simple reason: not doing so could translate into a loss on Election Day.

One thing to keep in mind, however, is that when exposure to Democrats' advertising is substantial, exposure to Republicans' advertising is often also quite substantial. This implies that when citizens see barrages of ads from both candidates, the realized impact is often zero. This is exactly what Zaller (1996) worried was masking real campaign effects. As we made clear in Chapter 3, however, there are often imbalances in exposure. This can happen because of citizens' viewing habits: perhaps a respondent in some media market tends to watch mostly game shows or talk shows, where the Democrat in that race may have aired more ads. Or it can happen because of more general campaign ad patterns: perhaps the Republican Senate or presidential candidate simply aired more ads in a respondent's market.

Can we say for certain that the elections studied in this chapter were won or lost on the basis of advertising? Not with the evidence presented thus far. Using the survey data, there are frequently too few voters in any given market or state for which we can simulate alternative outcomes of an election with different advertising scenarios. But because the effects are most often and most strongly felt in close races in which marginal effects can often change the dynamics of a race, it is likely true that the aggregate impact of ad exposure is central to the distribution of election outcomes. Put simply, in a political environment in which outcomes turn on a few thousand or even hundreds of votes, advertising may make the difference between winning and losing.

We can actually go a bit further than mere speculation on this last point. If we broaden our use of data beyond surveys, we can learn more about the role of political advertising in tipping close races. To further assess the impact of political advertising in recent presidential and Senate races, we created a dataset with the county as the unit of analysis. The advertising data are aggregated to the media market level and appended to the county file. Each of the more than 3,000 counties in the contiguous forty-eight states is assigned by Nielsen to one of 210 media markets. Because we have both county-level election returns and the market-level ad totals for 2008, we are able to include that year in our analyses, as well.

We estimated ordinary least squares regression models predicting Gore's percentage of the vote in the county in 2000, Kerry's percentage of the vote in 2004, and Obama's percentage of the vote in 2008. We did the same for Senate races in all three years, estimating the Democratic candidate's share of the vote.[11] The key independent variable in all of our models is a Democratic advertising advantage measure, which is simply the number of pro-Democratic ads (aired in the market in the final month of the campaign) minus the number of pro-Republican ads.

The results are compelling. Advertising had a significant impact on vote share in all six contexts. The full-model results are reported in Appendix B, but the important effect of note is what advertising contributed to the final outcome, and whether an alternative ad environment would have resulted in a different winner. In other words, would the outcome have changed if the losing candidate had been able to

---

[11] Each of our models also contains a series of socio-demographic measures (percent male, percent black, percent white, percent Asian, percent Hispanic, median income in the county, percent younger than twenty-five, and percent older than sixty-five), as well as the percent of the vote for the Democratic and Republican presidential candidates in the county in the previous election. In our presidential models, we include the number of candidates' visits to the media market in the fall campaign, and in our Senate models we control for incumbency and per capita spending by each candidate in the state.

TABLE 4.6 Simulated Voting and Election Changes

	With 10% increase in ad buys		With 15% increase in ad buys	
	No. of votes changed	States changed	No. of votes changed	States changed
2000 presidential	134,621	NM, FL, WI, OR	201,932	NM, FL, IA, WI, OR
2004 presidential	98,161	WI	147,242	NM, WI
2008 presidential	119,073	MO	178,609	MO, NC
2000 Senate	469,985	WA, MI	704,987	VA, WA, NE, MI
2004 Senate	404,807	FL	607,211	FL, KY
2008 Senate	243,425	MN	365,138	MN, OR, GA

Note: "Votes changed" are for an increase in Democrats' ad buys. "States changed" are for an increase by the losing candidate. Full model results from which these estimates are derived are included in Appendix B.

afford more advertising? Using the model estimates, we entered some hypothetical values indicating an ad advantage for one candidate. This produced an expected vote for each county, which was then aggregated to the state level.[12]

We show the simulated effects in two ways. First, how many votes would the Democratic candidates have gained with 10 percent or 15 percent more ads across all of the states in the presidential race and all of the Senate contests that year?[13] This might amount to a dozen more ads in some markets to upward of 300 or more ads in other markets. Second, within states, how many outcomes would have changed if the losing candidate had had the hypothetical boost in resources?

The results are reported in Table 4.6. Consider first the results in the 2000 presidential contest. With a 10 percent increase in pro-Gore ads, the vice-president would be expected to gain almost 135,000 votes nationwide. With a 15 percent increase in ads, the gain would be just over 200,000 votes. Several states would have given their Electoral

---

[12] Such an alternative reality is not so simplistic, of course. With fewer or greater resources, candidates might distribute their ads differently.

[13] This estimate of changed votes actually understates the true effect. For example, if the Democratic candidate is expected to gain 5,000 votes in a state (the estimate we show), the Republican is expected to lose about 5,000 votes (depending on the presence of any third-party threat). The net change for the Democrat, then, is 10,000 votes.

College votes to a different candidate had the ad environment been slightly different. Bush would have won New Mexico, Wisconsin, and Oregon with a 10 percent increase in ads in those states, and he would have won Iowa with a 15 percent increase in advertising. Gore would have won Florida and the White House had he increased his ad buys by 10 percent in the six major Florida markets.

A close look at the ad patterns in Florida in 2000 is instructive. In the entire state, the Bush campaign, including party and interest group allies, aired over 1,500 more ads in October than Al Gore and his supporters. The campaigns focused their resources in slightly different parts of the state, however. Gore held an advantage of over 800 ads in the Orlando and West Palm Beach media markets, which accounted for nearly 30 percent of the state's population, but Bush battered Gore in ads aired in Jacksonville (tripling Gore's ad buys), Mobile (which covers the panhandle), Miami, and Tampa. Had Gore decided on additional ad buys in the West Palm Beach market, which he won with 57 percent of the vote, or tried to engage more voters in Mobile or Jacksonville (both of which went heavily to Bush and both of which Gore largely conceded to him), he might have won the state.

The simulated change in advertising in October 2004 shifts a slightly lower number of votes nationwide than advertising in 2000 and only influences the outcome in one or two states (Wisconsin for Bush and New Mexico for Kerry). Neither change would have altered who became president. A lower number of states are at risk under this alternative because Kerry lost some close states by larger margins than Gore did in 2000 (Florida, Iowa, Missouri) and won other states by larger margins than Gore (Oregon and New Hampshire, the latter of which was a red state in 2000 by 7,000 votes but a blue state in 2004 by 9,000 votes).

The same is true for the Obama–McCain race in 2008. In many ways, this race was more interesting in that it was the first true open seat since 1952. In other ways, however, the election was less interesting. Despite a brief surge in the polls for the McCain camp after the nomination of Sarah Palin as vice-president and the GOP convention, Senator Obama led throughout. He ended up winning with 53 percent of the vote and 365 electoral votes. Still, advertising volumes are significantly related to county-level outcomes, and more than 100,000 votes are expected to have shifted with a modest 10 percent change in the number of ads aired.

Across the three presidential elections, in fact, the expected shift in votes is roughly comparable. Of course, the size of those shifts is relatively small when one considers that more than 100 million people cast ballots in each election, but even small vote shifts are critically important in close elections. Putting all three presidential races together, nine states would have switched from red to blue, or vice versa, given a 15 percent shift in campaign ad buys.

The Senate results in 2000, 2004, and 2008 are also suggestive of an advertising effect. A systematic surge in ad buys of 15 percent for the Democratic candidate across all Senate races could have gained the party anywhere from 360,000 votes in 2008 to just over 700,000 in 2000, amounting to a larger aggregate effect than in the presidential context. With only a 10 percent increase in ad buys for the losing candidate, however, only four states in all three years are expected to have flipped: the incumbent Republicans Slade Gorton of Washington and Spencer Abraham of Michigan would have defeated the challengers Maria Cantwell and Debbie Stabenow in 2000; the Democrat Betty Castor would have defeated the Republican Mel Martinez in the open-seat race in Florida in 2004; and the incumbent Republican Norm Coleman of Minnesota would have managed to defeat Al Franken in 2008.

It should be noted that a win for Gorton in Washington in 2000 would have affected the resulting balance of power in the Senate. Instead of a 50–50 Senate, the Republicans would have controlled the chamber 51–49. As a consequence, the defection of the Republican James Jeffords of Vermont in 2001 would not have switched the Senate to Democratic control. Furthermore, a win for Coleman in Minnesota in 2008 would have prevented a filibuster-proof Democratic majority, which held until Scott Brown won the special election in Massachusetts to replace Senator Ted Kennedy in early 2010. With a 15 percent increase in ads for the losing candidate, a total of nine Senate races in all three years were at risk.[14]

---

[14] Some might argue that our county-level models suffer from endogeneity. That is, candidates may put advertising into markets where they expect to do well. We took a number of approaches to account for this. First, we included control variables in all of our models

At the end of the day, however, we urge caution at drawing too deep an inference from these simulations. In all of the presidential states and Senate races where the simulation predicted an alternative outcome, the winning candidate won by a razor-thin margin. This implies, of course, that any change in campaign strategy by the losing candidate could have delivered the state to him or her. For example, if the candidate had invested in more get-out-the-vote efforts, given a stronger performance in debates, or avoided a gaffe, the outcome also might have been different. Our goal here is to demonstrate that ad buys are substantively and statistically related to voting outcomes and are but one additional and effective means by which to reach voters and draw them to your column. It may be true that such efforts work only at the margins, but close and consequential elections are decided at the margins, and every effort or missed opportunity can represent the difference between winning and losing.

Conclusion

We started the chapter with a set of expectations about the contexts under which campaign ads should matter the most. In general, we can draw the following inferences from our results. First, advertising is broadly effective—far more broadly than theory might suggest. Second, ads do seem to have a greater level of effectiveness in races in which the candidates are less well known. In our individual-level results, for example, the largest ad effects were for Senate challengers and open-seat candidates. In our county-level results, more votes were moved by Senate ads than by presidential ads. These findings hold up well across election cycles.

---

for presidential performance in the covered market in the previous election. Second, using the advice of Huber and Arceneaux (2007), we re-estimated the presidential models for non-battleground states, where advertising exposure is incidental and exogenous to previous vote. The results in the non-battleground states were still statistically significant. Finally, in our Senate models, we estimated a market-level model with Democrats' and Republicans' ads as the dependent variable and prior presidential vote in the market as an explanatory variable. In no case did prior performance predict ad buys for Senate candidates. Thus, it seems more likely that the identified relationships reported here are true causal ones.

We have only begun our investigation into the impact of televised political advertising, however. The set of analyses in this chapter has assumed that ad effects are similar across all types of voters and that an ad is an ad. That is, different types of ads are equally effective. The latter assumption is the one we investigate next. In Chapter 5, we ask whether the tone of the ad, and the emotions the ad seeks to elicit, make any difference in its effectiveness.

5 How Negativity and Emotional Appeals in Ads Matter

I **N OCTOBER 2007,** the Republican presidential candidate Mitt Romney launched an ad in Iowa in which he looked viewers in the eye and talked about the threat posed to the United States by "jihadism." He described "a violent, radical, Islamic fundamentalism" whose goal was to "unite the world under a single jihadist caliphate" by working to "collapse freedom-loving nations like us." The threat described by Romney is a scary one for most Americans, and his language is quite emotionally charged. Yet under the most common scheme used to categorize the tone of political ads, Romney's ad would be considered a positive one because it makes no mention of his opponents for the Republican nomination.

The following month, the Democratic candidate John Edwards aired an ad in New Hampshire that began with him proclaiming to the viewer: "This system is corrupt. And it's rigged. And it's rigged against you." It is certainly a bit startling to hear those lines introduce a political ad, and it is a proclamation that might even make some viewers angry or upset. Yet Edwards does not mention any of his Democratic opponents for the nomination, and so again the ad would be considered a positive one by almost any coding scheme.

These two examples of political ads serve to make an important point about the content and categorization of political ads. Namely, there is considerable variation across "positive" ads—and across "negative" ads, for that matter. Positive ads do not necessarily invoke happy thoughts, and sometimes they may even serve to elicit downright negative emotions among viewers, such as fear or anger. Is it appropriate, then, to lump together an upbeat ad in which a candidate speaks of his "family values" with one that speaks of a jihadist threat to America?

A wealth of studies have examined the specific impact of negative advertising on persuasion, but, as we showed in Chapter 2, the findings are often conflicting, with some suggesting that negativity has its intended impact and others suggesting that advertising leads to a backlash against the sponsor. Our premise in this chapter is that to understand the influence of political advertising, one may need to move beyond the traditional categorization of ads as positive or negative to consider the specific emotions that they elicit.

Indeed, political scientists increasingly have begun to question the typical positive–negative categorization of political advertising. Many, for example, have suggested adding a third category: the contrast ad (Jamieson, Waldman, and Sherr 2000). We adopt that approach in this chapter, distinguishing between ads that only mention an opponent and ads that compare the sponsor with the opponent. Others have proposed different categorizations altogether (ones we do not consider here), such as whether the ad could be considered mudslinging or not (Kahn and Kenney 1999), whether the ad is fair (Lawton and Freedman 2001), whether the ad is uncivil (Brooks and Geer 2007; Fridkin and Kenney 2008), and whether the ad is relevant to the election (Fridkin and Kenney 2008).

One characteristic that has not been studied much, however, is the specific emotional appeals that an ad contains. This is curious given that political scientists increasingly have been turning to emotion as an integral part of explanations of behavior. And as attention to emotions has increased, political scientists have developed new theories of political behavior in which emotion is central (Brader 2006; Marcus, Neuman, and MacKuen 2000). In light of this developing literature, we ask whether coding several specific emotional appeals contained within political advertising can provide better explanations for how political advertising influences voters' choices than can a traditional tone-based approach.

The Timing and Frequency of Negativity and Emotional Appeals

Of course, if emotional appeals are to have an impact on voters, they must be present in the campaign. Our data reveal, first and foremost, that emotional appeals not only are present in political advertising but are widespread.

For this chapter, we supplemented the Wisconsin Advertising Project's coding with coding of our own about the emotions elicited from each ad aired in 2004. Our investigation of the impact of emotions focuses solely on 2004, as we do not have access to the video versions of ads from 2000.[1] When we broaden our analysis later in the chapter to the impact of tone on voting choice, we are able to examine 2000, as well.

In coding the ads for emotional appeals, two coders were asked to report whether each ad was intended to produce any of five emotions: anger, fear, enthusiasm, pride, and compassion.[2] These were the five emotions that Brader (2006) found most frequently in political ads in the 2000 campaign. Coders were asked specifically, "Was the sponsor of this ad attempting to elicit [insert emotion]?"

The objective of this question was not to tap the emotional response of the coder but to allow the coder to independently judge the ad maker's goal in designing the message. Coders could respond by indicating the ad contained "no appeal" to the emotion, "some appeal," or a "strong appeal." We collapsed "some" and "strong" into one category, so that all ads that contained some element of each of the emotions examined were combined.[3] In general, the reliability of

---

[1] More specifically, our coders used the videos of each ad to assess the emotional appeal. Most other coding by the Wisconsin Advertising Project, especially in 2000, relied only on the printed storyboards of political ads. Using storyboards poses few coding problems for most content questions, including tone, but they are significantly inferior for questions about emotional appeals, which are often implicit in the music and voiceovers.

[2] The analysis in this chapter, and the discussion of the coding, refers only to ads aired during the general election. Primary election ads were excluded. Each of the two coders coded half of the ads. We met regularly with each coder to discuss potential issues and concerns.

[3] This coding structure follows the one outlined in Brader 2006, 148–152.

the coding was high,[4] but coders did have difficulty identifying compassion appeals. Moreover, in almost 90 percent of the cases where coders identified enthusiasm, they also reported the presence of a pride appeal. Because of that, we chose to drop pride and compassion from the analysis and focus on fear, anger, and enthusiasm.

Our primary goal in this research is to compare a traditional tone-based account of advertising's effects with a discrete emotions model. Does one model give more leverage than the other in understanding the impacts of political advertising on voting choice?

The first thing to establish is that negative ads are distinct from those that feature fear or anger, and that positive ads are distinct from those that feature enthusiasm appeals. Table 5.1 speaks to this by showing a cross-tabulation of ad tone and emotional appeal for the nearly 2 million Senate and presidential ads aired in 2004. The numbers are split into four subgroups—Senate Democrats, Senate Republicans, Bush, and Kerry—and the entries represent the percentage of ads by emotion that were classified as positive, negative, or contrast.

Although there is a strong relationship between the tone of advertising and its emotional content, there are also differences.[5] Take fear appeals, for instance. More than 70 percent of Bush's and Kerry's fear ads were negative, but the relationship was not nearly as strong for Senate candidates: Fifty-nine percent of Senate Democrats' fear ads were negative, and 41 percent of Senate Republicans' ads were. A substantial percentage of fear ads were even positive. For example, 21 percent of Senate Democrats' fear ads were positive, and 14 percent of Senate Republicans' fear ads were deemed by coders to be positive.

The presence of positive fear ads might seem strange, the Mitt Romney "Jihadist" ad notwithstanding, but there are other examples

---

[4] To assess inter-coder reliability, we had ten additional coders assess up to eighty random ads on each of the five emotions. Coders for the reliability test were trained in a one-hour session in which political ads from earlier cycles were viewed and discussed. We established the specific coding criteria and worked through a number of examples. For fear and anger, Pearson correlations on the three-category coding ranged between a low of 0.55 to a high of 0.82. For enthusiasm, correlations were even higher, ranging between 0.65 and 0.81.

[5] Keep in mind that when coders are asked to assess the tone of the ad, it is essentially an objective question. Negative ads are those that discuss only the opposing candidate; positive ads are those that discuss only the favored candidate; and contrast ads mention or show both candidates. This objective criterion has the virtue of minimizing coders' subjectivity, but it also masks what are surely important differences within the categories.

TABLE 5.1 Distribution of Tone within Emotional Appeals

	Attack	Contrast	Promote	No. of airings containing appeal	% of airings containing appeal
Senate Democrats					
Fear	0.59	0.20	0.21	45,257	0.37
Anger	0.45	0.39	0.16	71,043	0.58
Enthusiasm	0.01	0.24	0.75	81,376	0.66
Senate Republicans					
Fear	0.41	0.45	0.14	47,000	0.36
Anger	0.41	0.48	0.11	70,413	0.55
Enthusiasm	0.03	0.31	0.66	93,653	0.73
Kerry					
Fear	0.71	0.28	0.01	260,072	0.40
Anger	0.55	0.37	0.08	441,751	0.69
Enthusiasm	0.06	0.43	0.51	384,860	0.60
Bush					
Fear	0.72	0.18	0.09	269,293	0.66
Anger	0.81	0.19	0.00	298,623	0.73
Enthusiasm	0.00	0.40	0.60	141,242	0.35

Note: Entries are the proportion of ad airings by emotion that were negative, positive, or contrast.

of such ads. In 2004, the Democratic Senate candidate Betty Castor of Florida aired a positive ad titled "Terrorism." The ad featured Castor addressing the audience directly:

> Every candidate talks about terrorism, but I've dealt with it firsthand. As a university president, I took action to remove a suspected terrorist from our campus. And I saw how the failure to share information among agencies threatens the safety of our community. In the Senate, I'll use my experience to demand better intelligence and to strengthen local law enforcement. I'm Betty Castor, and I approved this message because to me fighting terrorism isn't just policy; it's personal.

The ad never mentions her opponent, making it a positive ad, but Castor also appeals directly to citizens' fears about terrorism and whether the country is prepared to meet that threat.

As for anger, 81 percent of Bush's anger ads were negative (i.e., focused on criticizing John Kerry), while only 55 percent of Kerry's anger ads were primarily focused on criticizing George Bush. In the Senate case, 45 percent of anger appeals from Democrats were negative, and 39 percent were contrast ads; a larger percentage of Republican anger appeals were found in contrast ads (48 percent) than in negative ads (41 percent).

In addition, although almost no enthusiasm ads were purely negative, 24–43 percent were contrast ads. In particular, Kerry and Bush were more likely to use contrast ads to convey enthusiasm than were Senate Democrats and Republicans. In all cases, however, a majority of enthusiasm appeals appeared in positive ads.

As with the presence of positive fear appeals, it may be useful to consider positive ads that do and do not contain enthusiasm. In 2004, Republican Senator Tom Coburn of Oklahoma, who is also a doctor, aired a positive ad called "Cancer Patient." In the ad, a mother recounts Coburn's diagnosis of her cancer while she was pregnant. She discusses the complications of her surgery, which was successful, and tells the viewing audience, "I'm so grateful to Dr. Tom." The screen then shows the name of Dr. Tom Coburn with the tagline, "He cared for her. He'll care for you." This ad certainly makes an appeal to compassion; an appeal to enthusiasm is not evident. That is not the case, however, in another of Coburn's ads, this one called "Decision," which is brimming with enthusiasm. Over the musical backdrop of a softly playing horn, Coburn tells an audience largely of senior citizens:

> The reason I want to go to Washington is not to be a U.S. senator. I want to go Washington to change America. To awaken it back to the real ideal on which we were founded: the American dream. And I believe our grandchildren and our children are worth changing the way things operate in Washington.

These examples are meant to illustrate the considerable diversity that exists within each tone category.

Finally, consider the last column of the table, which shows the percentage of all general election ads for each group that appealed to the three emotions. The distinctions between Senate Republicans and Democrats here were relatively slight. Both sets of candidates featured

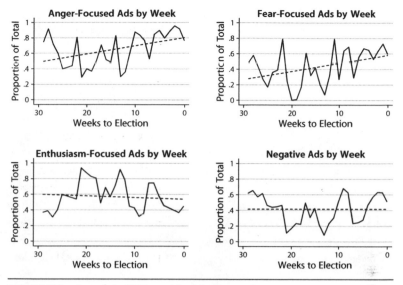

FIGURE 5.1 Appeals in 2004 presidential ads over time

fear appeals in a little over 33 percent of their ads; both featured anger appeals in just over half of their ads; and both featured enthusiasm appeals in about two-thirds of their aired spots.

Differences between Kerry and Bush, however, were much starker. Although the presidential candidates appealed to anger in about seven in ten ads (a strikingly high number), Kerry was far more likely to appeal also to enthusiasm. Sixty percent of his ads appealed to enthusiasm, compared with 35 percent of Bush's ads. Kerry also was much less likely to appeal to fear. Forty percent of his ads contained a fear appeal, while 66 percent of Bush's ads did.

It is also interesting to see how the use of these "big three" emotional appeals varied over time. Figure 5.1 shows the distribution of such appeals over the course of the presidential race. The upper left panel, for instance, shows the percentage of presidential ad airings in each week leading up to Election Day in which anger was invoked. Superimposed is a fitted regression line, which gives an indication of the trend over time. There is considerable variability from week to week, but in general, the closer one gets to Election Day, the more anger ads that were aired. In fact, there is one period from nine to twelve weeks before the election in which nearly 90 percent of the ad airings in the presidential race contained an appeal to anger.

The use of fear appeals in the presidential race also increased as Election Day approached. The percentage of total appeals of this type, however, was lower than the percentage of anger appeals, averaging about 40 percent of total ads in a given week. Enthusiasm appeals were evident in every part of the campaign, apparent in about 60 percent of ads for a given week. Though no real linear trend is evident in the use of such appeals over time, it does appear that the use of enthusiasm appeals is highest during the middle of the campaign.

The pattern of negative ad use, however, does not reflect the over-time distribution of ads that contained emotional appeals. Although the regression line describing negativity over time is flat, it is evident from the lower right panel in Figure 5.1 that negativity seemed to peak early in the campaign—twenty-five to thirty weeks before Election Day—and in the weeks closest to Election Day.

The use of emotional appeals was not quite as common in the 2004 U.S. Senate races, as Figure 5.2 shows. Ads featuring anger appeals constituted about 45 percent of the ad airings in an average week, and fear ads were comparatively rare, making up about 20 percent of the ad airings in any week. Moreover, negative ads were much less common than in the presidential race of 2004.

By contrast, enthusiasm appeals in the Senate races were just as common, if not more so, than in the presidential race. In contrast to the presidential race, the regression lines indicating the trend in the use of each appeal over time, while increasing, are mostly flat. In fact, closer inspection of the data in Figure 5.2 reveals some nonlinearities, with a U-shaped pattern of anger ad airings and negative ad airings.

In sum, emotional appeals in political advertising are quite common, with anger appeals ubiquitous in Senate ads and especially in presidential ads. Enthusiasm appeals are also quite common but are even more so in Senate ads. Finally, the use of the "big three" emotional appeals generally increases over time, although some appeals are used frequently even in the very early stages of the campaign, almost thirty weeks before Election Day.[6]

---

[6] Although explaining why certain appeals are used at certain points in the campaign would be an interesting endeavor—for example, whether emotions are used in response to campaign events or poll numbers—it is beyond the scope of our analysis.

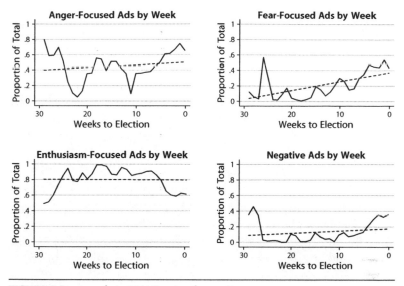

FIGURE 5.2   Appeals in 2004 Senate ads over time

More generally, given how common emotional appeals in advertising are throughout the campaign, and given that the discrete emotional appeals examined here do not perfectly coincide with the traditional conception of tone, we expect the persuasive effects of ad tone to be different from the persuasive effects of emotional appeals.

Expectations

Our review of the literature in Chapter 2 suggests four competing models about how the characteristics of advertising—whether tone or emotional appeals—will have an impact on the effectiveness of advertising in changing people's minds.

The first model is what we labeled the intended effects model, in which exposure to negative advertising, as its sponsor intended, should lower evaluations of the attacked candidate, leading to a greater likelihood of voting for the sponsor of the ad. Likewise, exposure to positive advertising should increase evaluations of the ad's sponsor, increasing the likelihood of voting for the sponsoring candidate.

Our second model, the backlash effects model, is also tone-based and suggests that exposure to negative ads turns voters against the sponsor of the ad; thus, the likelihood of voting for the attacked candidate should actually increase.

Our third model, which we have labeled the affect transfer account emphasizes the emotional content of ads and suggests that exposure to ads that induce fear, anger, or any other negative emotion should have the same directional effect as exposure to negative ads. Likewise, exposure to enthusiasm or other positive emotional appeals should have the same impact as exposure to positive ads.

We call the final model the discrete emotions model. Under this model, different emotional appeals should have different effects on voters. As suggested by affective intelligence theory, fear ads should lead to vigilance and thus lead opinions to change. Anger ads, by contrast, should not lead opinions to change, as information processing may shut down when people get angry. Finally, enthusiasm appeals should lead to stronger support among those who already support the ad's sponsor, but they should have no impact on those who do not initially support the ad's sponsor.

The Impact of Ad Tone

To investigate the relationship between ad characteristics and voting choice, we examined the 2000 and 2004 presidential and U.S. Senate races. As described in Chapter 3, our source of public opinion data in 2000 was the ANES; in 2004, it was the three-wave BYU–UW survey. Unlike in Chapter 4, we restrict our analysis to the general elections of 2000 and 2004, and we make no distinctions between race contexts for the analysis of Senate races. We begin in this section with a focus on the tone of ads.

We should restate that our focus is on exposure to the entire set of negative, contrast, and positive ads—not on exposure to a specific ad or set of ads. It may very well be true, for example, that a specific negative ad will result in backlash against the sponsor among voters, but with more abundant, and more effective, negative ads, that effect could be mitigated or overcome. We are explicitly interested, then, in whether the entire ad environment seen by voters influences evaluations of candidates and voting behavior—the effect of ultimate concern to candidates and consultants.

Using the coded ad data, we merged the frequency of different advertising appeals by media market onto the surveys noted above. Because our primary interest is in the effects of ad tone and emotional appeals in each ad, we created separate measures of exposure to ads featuring each of the three emotions and tones. Each model contains four exposure measures: Democratic and Republican ads of a specific tone, and Democratic and Republican ads without that tone. We take the same approach in models estimating the impact of emotional appeals by creating measures of Democratic and Republican exposure to the specific emotional appeal and measures of Democratic and Republican exposure to all remaining ads (i.e., those without the specific emotional appeal of interest).

We estimate the impact of ad content on reported voting choice, measured as a simple dichotomous variable (vote for the Democratic or Republican U.S. Senate and presidential candidate). We also estimate the influence of ad exposure on voters' evaluations of candidates (i.e., favorability scores), as we did in Chapter 4. Because the inclusion of these latter models would triple the amount of statistical evidence in this chapter, we do not discuss these models in depth here. Interested readers may turn to Appendix C for partial results of these favorability models, but it is safe to say that, in general, the pattern of findings for the favorability models is very similar to the pattern for the voting choice models.

Ad exposure is our key independent variable, but all of our models contain the same predictors used in Chapter 4, including respondents' demographics (educational attainment, age, gender, race, income, marital status, and region of residence) and attitudes (party identification and approval of the president).[7]

Table 5.2 shows how exposure to a candidate's positive, contrast, and negative ads has an impact on the likelihood of voting for the Democratic candidate in the presidential and Senate races in 2000 and

[7] Unlike for Chapter 4, however, we do not report full-model results in an appendix, principally because the key difference in all of the models in this chapter is the disaggregation of exposure into tone or emotion-based classifications. Thus, the control variables barely change in size or substantive significance from the results reported in Appendix B. This will be similarly true in Chapter 6, where the key difference in the models is the split of exposure into various respondent-based subgroups.

TABLE 5.2 Impact of Ad Exposure on Voting Choice by Ad Tone

	Democratic exposure			Republican exposure		
	Negative	Contrast	Positive	Negative	Contrast	Positive
2000 Senate:	−0.091	**0.177**	0.059	0.115	−0.085	−0.130
Vote Democratic	(−0.68)	**(1.71)**	(0.57)	(1.02)	(−1.08)	(−1.51)
2004 Senate:	−0.062	−0.174	0.305	**−0.148**	**0.313**	**−0.460**
Vote Democratic	(−0.500)	(−1.18)	(1.36)	**(−1.83)**	**(1.88)**	**(−1.98)**
2000 presidential:	−0.127	0.378	**0.387**	−0.124	−0.019	−0.291
Vote Gore	(−0.540)	(1.51)	**(1.69)**	(−0.390)	(−0.100)	(−1.16)
2004 presidential:	0.285	0.255	−0.157	**−0.832**	−0.083	−0.301
Vote Kerry	(1.26)	(0.79)	(−0.45)	**(−2.25)**	(−0.038)	(−1.08)

Survey: 2000 ANES and 2004 BYU–UW panel study.

Note: Entries are coefficients with *z*-scores (in parentheses). Models are estimated using logit. Bold-face indicates that the variable is statistically significant at the .10 level. The boxed coefficients represent the results of one model estimation. Each similarly paired coefficient within tone is from one model run. The models also contain Democratic and Republican exposure to all ads not of that tone. Those exposure results and all other control variables are not shown here.

2004. We report the coefficients and *z*-scores from separate models predicting voting choice: one with exposure to Democratic and Republican negative ads included separately; one with exposure to each party's contrast ads; and one with exposure to each party's positive ads. Recall that a *z*-score is simply an indicator of how likely it is that a relationship could have occurred by chance, with *z*-scores above 1.64 or below −1.64 providing fairly good evidence that a relationship is a true one.

The results in the presidential races are most consistent with an intended effects explanation. In 2000, exposure to Democrats' positive ads increases the likelihood of voting for Gore, which is the only statistically significant effect of advertising that we observe in that year's presidential race. Exposure to Gore's contrast ads, however, is close to being a statistically significant predictor of vote choice. None of George Bush's ads that year—positive, negative, or contrast—made any noticeable difference on respondents' reported voting choice.

Compare these findings with the effects of total advertising on presidential voting choice reported in Chapter 4, where exposure to neither Gore's nor Bush's advertising mattered (the first row of Table 4.1). We see in this chapter that total exposure actually masked impor-

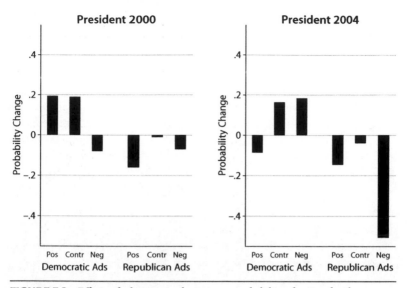

FIGURE 5.3 Effects of ad exposure by tone on probability of voting for the Democratic presidential candidate

Note: Each paired Democratic and Republican exposure effect (i.e., for negative ads) is the result of one model specification, where we vary exposure by one standard deviation. The effects for demographic and attitudinal control variables are not shown. Pos, positive; Contr, contrast; Neg, negative.

tant tone-based differences for Gore. While Gore's direct attacks on Bush had no effect on voting choice, his promotional spots and contrast spots did have some impact. This disaggregation is important, then, in unearthing the influence of advertising.

In the 2004 presidential race, we find that only Republicans' ads were effective, and it was their attack ads that drove voting choice. Increased exposure to Bush's negative ads increased the likelihood of voting for Bush ($z = -2.25$). There is no evidence of a backlash for either candidate in running negative ads.

Overall, the story in these findings is an intended effects one, as Figure 5.3 makes clear. This figure shows the impact on the probability of voting for the Democratic candidate of a change in exposure from one-half standard deviation below the mean to one-half standard deviation above the mean. With two exceptions (and these were cases in which the coefficient was not statistically significant), exposure to

Democrats' advertising increased the chances of voting for the Democratic candidate, and exposure to Republicans' advertising lowered those chances. That said, differences across years in the impact of ad tone complicate a narrative about the types of ads that work most consistently. Gore got a boost from positive ads in 2000. Note also that the effect of his contrast ads was noteworthy in size, even though the coefficient was marginally insignificant. Bush seems not to have swayed voters with his ads in 2000, but his attacks in 2004 were effective. The inconsistency of these findings across years suggests that the larger electoral context—events in the campaign, the issues being discussed in debates or in the media—may help to determine the impact of negative and positive ads.

In the Senate race models, also shown in Table 5.2, the intended effects model still holds up as the best explanation of how advertising works—although there is a bit more variation in our findings. In 2000, exposure to Democrats' contrast ads made respondents more likely to support the Democratic Senate candidate, but this was the only significant advertising effect in that year. Exposure to Senate Republicans' positive ads does come close, however. In the 2004 Senate races, we find no significant effects of advertising on the Democratic side, but exposure to Republican advertising did influence voting choice. Consistent with the intended effects explanation, exposure to both positive and negative advertising decreased the likelihood that someone would vote for the Democratic Senate candidate. But there is also one instance of a statistically significant backlash in that increased exposure to Republicans' contrast ads in 2004 lowered the likelihood of supporting the Republican candidate.

Taken as a whole, the ad tone results from the presidential and Senate models in 2000 and 2004 suggest that, far from turning scores of voters against their sponsors, ads are having the effects that their sponsors intend, and this is true regardless of whether the ad is positive, negative, or contrast. Indeed, of the four statistically significant effects in both years, three demonstrated increased support for the ad's sponsor. Thus, the intended effects model better fits the ad-tone data than the backlash effects model. Furthermore, as can be seen in Appendix C, ten coefficients are significant in the tone-based models predicting candidate favorability. All ten are intended effects.

On the other hand, there is just no consistent pattern of effects whereby ads of a particular tone are the best predictor of how people vote. Sometimes negative ads work; sometimes positive ads work; and sometimes contrast ads work. Keep in mind, though, that this scattered set of findings is echoed in existing literature on negative campaigns more generally. Because of this, we wonder whether a better explanation of how the characteristics of advertising influence voting choice might come from dividing up ads not by their tone but by the specific emotional appeals they make.

The Impact of Emotional Appeals

The approach we take in this section is to re-estimate all of our models, substituting measures of exposure to varying emotional appeals for our tone-based exposure measures. Recall that we have a number of different expectations about the impact of specific emotional appeals. We had expected that fear ads would be quite effective in moving voting choice because they would induce information processing—that is, make voters think and possibly reconsider their choices. But we also wondered whether anger ads might shut down voters' processing, which implies that anger appeals would be ineffective in moving votes. Table 5.3 shows the results from three separate models (one for each emotion). We report coefficient estimates along with z-scores.

TABLE 5.3 Impact of Ad Exposure on Voting Choice by Emotional Appeal

	Democratic exposure			Republican exposure		
	Fear	Enthusiasm	Anger	Fear	Enthusiasm	Anger
2004 Senate: Vote Democratic	**−0.162** **(−2.06)**	**0.421** **(2.13)**	**−0.153** **(−2.38)**	−0.108 (−0.530)	0.001 (0.01)	0.223 (1.28)
2004 presidential: Vote Kerry	**0.598** **(3.82)**	0.09 (0.37)	**0.552** **(3.02)**	−0.305 (−1.42)	−0.305 (−1.30)	−0.378 (−1.31)

Survey: 2000 ANES and 2004 BYU–UW panel study.

Note: Entries are coefficients with z-scores (in parentheses). Models are estimated using logit. Boldface indicates that the variable is statistically significant at the .10 level. The boxed coefficients represent the results of one model estimation. Each similarly paired coefficient within emotion is from one model run. The models also contain Democratic and Republican exposure to all ads not of that emotion. Those exposure results and all other control variables are not shown here.

In sum, we find particularly widespread emotion-based effects for Democrats' ads in both the presidential and Senate races—much more widespread than those found in the tone-based models—but this does not hold true for Republicans' ads. Exposure to Republicans' fear, anger, and enthusiasm ads, whether presidential or Senate, had little impact on the choices that voters were making. For exposure to Bush ads, however, it should be noted that the three coefficient estimates are in the expected direction and approach conventional levels of statistical significance.

There is an important difference in the Democratic presidential and Senate results, however. Kerry's fear ads were effective in drawing voters to him in the presidential race, but Democrats' fear ads in the Senate races that year increased the likelihood that they would vote for a Republican. This is similarly true for Democratic anger ads. Put simply, exposure to some Democrats' appeals was, in fact, working against Democratic Senate candidates that year. One should keep in the mind, however, the initial pattern of results from the previous chapter, which showed that advertising as a whole tends to move Democrats and Republicans into their respective camps. This implies that the intended effects of Democrats' messages for Senate candidates in 2004 overwhelmed the backlash effects of their fear and anger appeals, all else being equal. But it also implies that Senate Democrats are likely to have done even better by avoiding fear and anger appeals in their ads.

Figure 5.4 shows the magnitude of the impact of exposure to each type of appeal, changing exposure from one-half standard deviation below the mean of respondents in our dataset to one-half standard deviation above. In the presidential race, the use of emotional appeals was doing what its sponsors intended, and the size of the effects was large. The direction and size of ad effects are dissimilar in U.S. Senate races, however.

What might explain the backlash effects for Senate Democrats? One explanation might be the somewhat different focus of Senate Democrats' fear and anger appeals compared with the focus of their Republican opponents. For example, one additional code in our dataset of political advertisements is whether an ad was primarily focused on policy issues, the personal traits of the candidates, or a mixture of

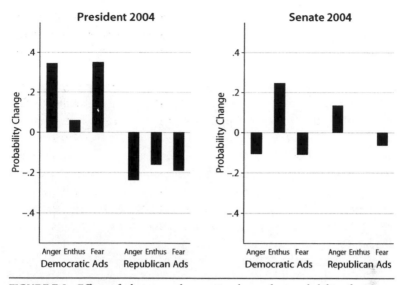

FIGURE 5.4 Effects of ad exposure by emotional appeal on probability of voting for the Democratic candidate

Note: Each paired Democratic and Republican exposure effect (i.e., for anger ads) is the result of one model specification, where we vary exposure by one standard deviation. The effects for demographic and attitudinal control variables are not shown. Enthus, enthusiasm.

both. For Senate Democrats in 2004, roughly 20 percent of fear and anger appeals were focused on candidates' traits, compared with only 13 percent of the Republicans' ads. This is evident in an ad from Florida in which Betty Castor accuses her opponent, Mel Martinez, of "more lies and hypocritical attacks" in regard to a suspected terrorist who was employed by the University of South Florida, of which Castor had been president. Or consider an ad from Washington State in which Patty Murray attacks her opponent, George Nethercutt, for reversing his stand on term limits: "A professional politician who will do anything to get elected," the narrator says against a backdrop of newspaper ads criticizing the Republican. Notably, in the presidential race, such personal attacks in fear and anger appeals were almost nonexistent. Fewer than 5 percent of Bush's and Kerry's fear and anger appeals were primarily about character traits, and more than three-quarters focused primarily on policy issues. At the end of the day, however, pure character attacks still only account for about one in five of all Senate ads, so the differences noted above between Republicans and Democrats may not entirely explain the backlash effects.

Another consideration is the context in which certain ad appeals work and when they do not. For example, 2004 was generally a pro-Republican year with respect to Senate races. The GOP won six seats previously held by Democratic senators. In contrast, the Democrats pried only two seats away from the GOP. It might be the case that the larger political environment was less conducive for Democrats' messages evoking fear and anger, especially lower down the ticket. We tested for this by interacting the fear and anger exposure measures in ways identical to the approach taken in Chapter 4. This allows us to compare the effects of ad exposure in different race contexts. The results show a tendency for Senate Democratic *incumbents* to suffer the largest backlash from fear and anger appeals.[8]

Our review of the literature also led us to believe that enthusiasm ads would draw voters to the candidate sponsoring the ad, though much theorizing suggests that this will only be true among citizens predisposed to vote for the sponsoring candidate. That is, Republicans' enthusiasm ads may increase the likelihood that someone who already supports a Republican candidate will vote for that candidate on Election Day, but such ads should have no impact on voters who favored the Democratic candidate before the election. The data we have presented to this point are not ideally suited to speaking to this idea because we do not separate respondents by whom they supported initially, but our findings do hint that the potential for enthusiasm appeals to work is not all that great. Only in one instance—with Democrats' ads in the 2004 Senate races—do enthusiasm ads influence voting choice.

Still, because our results may be concealing ad effects that show up only among certain subgroups of votes, we re-estimated our models separately for those who already supported the Democratic candidate

---

[8] We also wondered whether the issue focus of Senate ads across party might hold some key to explaining the backlash effects we noted. This does not seem to be case, however. In general, Senate Democrats primarily focused their fear and anger appeals on social welfare issues, while Senate Republicans tended to discuss foreign policy. This is consistent with the research on issue ownership, which suggests that candidates will campaign on those issues on which their party has a reputation for being able to handle well. It does not explain the backlash effects, however, because a similar pattern was noted for Kerry and Bush.

in the pre-election wave of the survey and for those who already supported the Republican candidate. We should be clear here: This test is informed directly from predictions in affective intelligence theory, which suggests that prior support moderates the effects of certain emotional appeals (Brader 2006). In reality, then, this is also a specific test for receiver-based effects. Because that is the focus of the next chapter, we keep this discussion to a minimum here.

In short, the results for the Senate races in 2004 are consistent with the theory that enthusiasm ads work best among existing supporters of a candidate. Democrats' enthusiasm ads work in firming up the support of existing Democratic supporters ($z = 1.69$), increasing the likelihood they will eventually vote for the Democratic candidate. This same pattern is true for exposure to Republicans' enthusiasm ads, which have no impact on supporters of the Democratic candidate but do increase the chances that supporters of the Republican candidate will eventually vote for her ($z = -3.49$). This suggests that appeals to enthusiasm can have the effect of "rallying the faithful," as Brader (2006, 144) notes.

The left panel of Figure 5.5 gives a visual depiction of these findings, revealing the sizeable magnitude of the impact of Democrats' enthusiasm ads on the supporters of Democratic candidate between the pre-election and post-election waves of the survey. Increasing exposure to Democrats' enthusiasm ads by one standard deviation results in a predicted increase in the probability of voting for the Democratic candidate of more than 0.3. The effect of the same change in exposure to Republicans' enthusiasm ads on Republicans is much less (about a 0.1 increase in the probability of voting for the Republican) but still noteworthy.

This pattern of findings with regard to enthusiasm ads does not extend to the presidential contest, however. In this race, the only statistically significant effect of enthusiasm appeals is an unanticipated one: initial Kerry supporters were less likely to vote for the Democratic nominee when exposed to increasing numbers of Bush enthusiasm appeals, implying that the president's ads softened support for his Democratic opponent. The size of the impact is considerable, as the right panel in Figure 5.5 reveals. Although this finding was unexpected, there may have been something about Bush's use of enthusiasm appeals in 2004—perhaps just an attempt to associate himself with

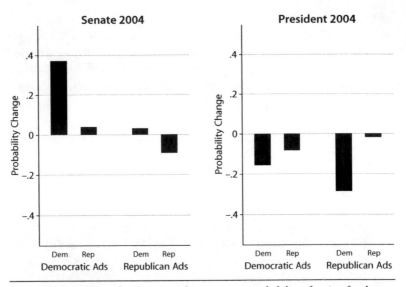

FIGURE 5.5 Effects of enthusiasm ad exposure on probability of voting for the Democratic candidate

Note: The bars show the change in probability of voting for the Democratic candidate, varying ad exposure by one standard deviation, for respondents who expressed support for the Democratic or Republican candidate in their pre-election interview. Dem, Democratic candidate; Rep, Republican candidate.

the presidency and country—that moved some initial Kerry supporters in his direction. As noted in Table 5.1, Bush made such appeals in only one of every three ads he aired.

So how well do the emotions-based models perform? Unfortunately, there is no additional clarity with an emotions-based classification of political ads. The affect transfer model, in which negative emotional appeals reduce support for a candidate and positive emotional appeals increase that support, fits the data in some instances (Kerry's ads), but not in others (Democratic Senate candidates). Nor do the expectations of our discrete emotions model fit the data particularly well. In fact, anger worked in much the same way as fear.

We can add that these divergent patterns are also present in our models predicting candidate evaluations (see Appendix C). There, Kerry's fear and anger ads boosted his favorability, and only Bush's enthusiasm ads were effective in moving evaluations of Bush. Senate Republicans saw some gains in favorability as a result of their anger and enthusiasm appeals, but Senate Democrats experienced a voter backlash when they used fear appeals.

Discussion

We began this research asking whether theories of emotion could do better than traditional theories that categorize ads as positive and negative in explaining the effect of political advertising on voting choice. To be clear, finding a consistent pattern of results is a high bar for questions of this sort. Dozens of existing studies reach different conclusions about the effects of ad tone on people's evaluations of candidates and voting choices. We had hoped that an emotions-based classification and a non-experimental research design might clear up the inconsistency, but that was not the case.

We can establish one narrative, however. The balance of evidence in this chapter suggests support for the intended effects model. In other words, of all the statistical findings in this chapter, we locate only three statistically significant instances of backlash—Republican Senate contrast ads in 2004 and Democratic Senate fear and anger ads that year. In all other instances—both presidential election years and for Senate candidates in 2000 and 2004—we located strong intended effects. This was true both in the tone-based and emotions-based classification of ads.

There is one practical reason to believe that exposure to ads generally and discrete classifications of ads specifically have their intended effects. Most campaign consultants are experienced and, we dare say, know what they are doing. Years of campaigning, combined with focus-group testing of potential ads, should provide them with at least some information about which ads are likely to be effective and not result in a voter backlash. Of course, campaigns can never know for sure whether an ad will resonate with viewers, but taken as a whole, the ads aired during an election should generate more support for their sponsor—that is, have an intended effect. Poorly designed ads that might turn off the public are likely to be dwarfed in number by ads that have an intended effect.

And candidates would very likely pull ads that seem to correlate with declines in poll numbers. That such decisions can happen in real time and with frequent polling means that a post-election assessment of ad exposure, like the one we conduct here, should not reveal much evidence of a backlash. That we find backlashes in Senate races but not the presidential elections might additionally confirm this. Presidential candidates have the resources necessary to develop ads with a low potential for backlash, whereas Senate candidates typically have less money to devote to message testing and have campaign managers who might be less adept at message crafting than the "big guns" who run presidential campaigns.

Note also that this explanation allows backlash ads to "wash out" in the aggregate—in contrast to a specific ad that candidates may use to secure publicity or free press. The latter ads are usually the most incendiary and negative and perhaps most likely to result in back-lashes. Ironically, as candidates use them to score free press, they open themselves up to more negative consequences because the ads cannot be pulled quickly from television stations. Thus, we might expect backlashes to occur more often when ads are replayed and commented on in news media coverage, as opposed to being seen only during commercial breaks. We consider this more explicitly in Chapter 7.

Although we have found fairly consistent support for the intended effects hypothesis, we did not have as much success in finding one type of ad that always broke through with voters. On this score, we cannot produce a compelling conclusion. We are simply unable to say with confidence that negative ads, or enthusiasm ads or anger ads produce the best return for the sponsoring candidate. We should also note that we considered the possible effects of other types of ad content—a possibility suggested by some new and developing research in this area (i.e., Fridkin and Kenney 2008; Geer 2006). For example, we also tested whether ads that feature purely policy-based attacks were more consistently successful, or whether character-based attacks were more likely to result in backlashes. We hinted at this last possibility in our discussion of the Senate Democratic backlash effects for fear and anger appeals in 2004.[9] Suffice it to say that the consideration of still more

---

[9] Indeed, if we estimate a model for Senate voting choice in 2004, when exposure to Senate Democrats' and Republicans' character attacks are the key independent variable (regardless of emotional appeal), the coefficient estimate for the Democrats is negative (suggesting a backlash) but statistically insignificant.

ad content codes does little to add clarity, especially when looking at multiple campaigns across election cycles. Of course, the larger message may be that there simply is no ad type that consistently works. Some types of ads may work in some races and years and not in others.

One thing is clear, though. Tone and emotional appeals are not one and the same. An anger appeal can be found in negative, contrast, and even positive advertising, and enthusiasm appeals pop up in negative ads on occasion. Ultimately, we believe that examining specific emotional appeals has promise, but it will be important for future researchers to back up such analyses with additional theory—specifically, theory about the context in which certain types of appeals are likely to work and when they are not—and data. We have said little, for example, about whether fear and anger appeals might be more or less effective for Senate challengers, incumbents, or open-seat candidates or whether an ad that invokes the specter of "jihadism" might be more or less effective in years in which the public believes that terrorism is a huge problem facing the country.

At the same time, of course, other classifications of ad content are worth additional investigation. We remain committed to the notion that ad persuasion is moderated by the types of ads viewers see. This is absolutely true based on the results we saw in this chapter, given that in some races positive ads were more effective than negative ads, and vice versa. But more work is needed to establish whether a certain type of ad is always or usually more effective than an alternative classification.

In the next chapter, we shift gears, turning our attention away from how differences in the content of the advertising matter and toward how differences in the characteristics of the ad's receiver (is the individual a strong partisan or not? is she knowledgeable about politics or not?) influence the persuasiveness of political advertising.

6 ▷ How Receivers' Characteristics Matter

DURING THE FALL 2004 presidential election, two major controversies rocked the political world. The first involved a *60 Minutes II* story aired on September 8, 2004, about George W. Bush's service in the National Guard in the late 1960s. The story claimed that Bush's father, the Republican Congressman George H. W. Bush, pulled strings to get his son into the Texas National Guard, thereby shielding him from being drafted to serve in Vietnam. The broadcast produced a significant backlash, however, when some alleged that the documents used to verify the report were not genuine. In the days following the broadcast, CBS was unable to convincingly prove that the documents were real. In the aftermath of the 2004 election, an independent panel determined that *60 Minutes* had not followed "basic journalistic principles" in investigating the story, leading the reporter, Dan Rather, to retire from CBS News after more than forty years with the network (Steinberg and Carter 2005).

The second controversy involved the Vietnam service of John Kerry, Bush's opponent in 2004. A collection of Vietnam veterans formed a group that year called Swift Boat Veterans for Truth and sponsored thousands of television ads challenging Kerry's patriotism and military service (Franz, Rivlin, and Goldstein 2006). In one particularly memorable ad, which aired in late September, an announcer told viewers, against the backdrop of images of a youthful John Kerry and Jane Fonda:

> Even before Jane Fonda went to Hanoi to meet with the enemy and mock America, John Kerry secretly met with enemy leaders in Paris, though we were still at war and Americans were being held in North Vietnamese prison camps. Then he returned and accused American troops of committing war crimes on a daily basis. Eventually, Jane Fonda apologized for her activities, but John Kerry refuses to. In a time of war, can America trust a man who betrayed his country?

We highlight these two controversies because they represent a fundamental difference in the *type* of political information that voters encounter during a political campaign; in short, some is quite complicated, while some is easy to understand. For our purposes in this book, we believe that different types of voters should respond in unique ways to the *60 Minutes* story and Swift Boat ads. The National Guard report, for example, and the ensuing controversy over its veracity, represents complicated political information with a number of subplots. One involved Bush's entry into the National Guard. Another involved his absence from a physical during his stint in Georgia. Some of the supporting characters in the story had died twenty years earlier, and some were still close friends of the Bush family. Most important, the basics of the story were conveyed chiefly through punditry on cable news, in print media, and on blogs. Thus, it was a story that was likely difficult for those who are low in political knowledge to comprehend. Indeed, a Gallup poll in late September 2004 reported that only 22 percent of Americans were paying "very close" attention to the story.[1]

In contrast, the Swift Boat Veterans spelled out quite clearly the narrative they hoped to convey: John Kerry had lied about his military service, and he betrayed his fellow American soldiers by protesting the war when he returned to America. To be fair, this story had some complicated elements, as well. It was, for instance, nearly thirty years old,

---

[1] The same poll found that 35 percent of respondents reported paying "not much" or "no" attention to the controversy, while 43 percent reported paying "some" attention to the story. Retrieved from the "Gallup Brain" search engine, at, http://brain.gallup.com/home .aspx, on April 10, 2008.

and it was debated ad nauseam on cable and talk radio. But unlike the Texas National Guard story, the Swift Boat narrative was contained in attractive thirty- and sixty-second ads that were hard to ignore and easy to understand—even for those with low levels of political knowledge.

Consider this: between September 1 and Election Day, the *New York Times* ran ninety-four stories that contained some reference to the Swift Boat Veterans. It featured fifty stories that made note of *60 Minutes'* National Guard report. On CNN, Fox News, and MSNBC, the Swift Boat Veterans were noted 400 times, while the National Guard story was discussed 255 times.[2] Both stories received ample news coverage. In the television air war, however, the Swift Boat Veterans aired just under 10,000 anti-Kerry attack ads. The Bush National Guard controversy, by contrast, was mentioned in only one ad, sponsored by Moveon.org, that aired only 200 times.[3]

For years, scholars have investigated whether certain types of voters are better able to understand and process campaign information. We noted in Chapter 2 that those who are low in political awareness are seen as having the hardest time understanding and integrating political information, though they are not immune to influence if a message is particularly intense. But we have argued that certain types of messages—namely, television ads—may also break through to low-information voters. Because television ads are packaged attractively and aired repeatedly, we expect that even those who are low in political information will be open to their influence.

In other words, while we accept that those who are low in political knowledge may be less likely to *understand and process* television ads, we expect the difference between political novices and the politically aware in this regard to be relatively slight. Consequently, because reception of a message is a precondition for accepting it, we have good reason to believe that these low-information viewers might even be *more* likely to be swayed by political advertising than their fellow citizens who are more politically aware—and who can more easily counter the information in ads. We take up this hypothesis, which we term the knowledge hypothesis, in this chapter.

---

[2] These figures are from a Lexis–Nexis search.

[3] The ad was titled "Swift Response," and it aired in four media markets (Toledo, Green Bay, Charleston, and Youngstown) between August 17 and August 21—notably, three weeks before CBS aired its report and spawned the uprising over its reporting.

In addition, we explore the moderating influence of partisanship. We expect that partisans, equipped with pre-existing political orientations, are better prepared to reject message that are inconsistent with their political predispositions. By contrast, political independents, because they are unlikely to resist the messages of any candidate as being inconsistent with their existing beliefs, will be influenced by exposure to advertising from both candidates. Stated differently, Democrats' advertising will have little impact on Republicans, but it *will* increase support for the sponsor among Democrats and independents. The same applies to Republicans' advertising, which is predicted to have its greatest impact on political independents and Republicans. Thus, one effect of the campaign—in addition to affecting independents—is to bring partisans home. We call this the partisanship hypothesis.

Consider how this partisanship hypothesis plays out given exposure to the Swift Boat advertisements. Certainly, their ability to persuade someone to vote against John Kerry depended on the person's partisanship. A strong Republican was likely to be sympathetic to and willing to accept the message that Kerry was unfit for the presidency. Thus, exposure to this ad likely made Republicans, who were already highly likely to vote for Bush, even more likely to do so. A Democrat, by contrast, although able to understand the message, was likely to reject it out of hand. Political independents had no dog in the fight, so not only did they take in the ad's anti-Kerry message, but there was little reason for them to reject the message. Thus, independents should have been most open to the ad's influence.

We saw in previous chapters that ads are effective in many political contexts (e.g., during primaries and in open-seat races), but that effects are dependent also on the content of the ad (in both tone and emotional appeal). In this chapter, we switch our focus to explore the moderating influence of viewers' characteristics, focusing in particular on levels of political knowledge and partisanship. Of course, these are not the only characteristics that might make individuals more or less susceptible to the influence of advertising. Perhaps men and women respond differently to the same ad, or perhaps age plays a role. That said, knowledge and partisanship are most noted by past researchers as influencing how well ads work, so we consider only these two factors. Our focus on such differences is a crucial element in our overall story and one that further clarifies when and to what extent political ads can influence elections.

The Moderating Effect of Political Information

We investigate the same dependent variables that we did in the previous chapters: Senate and presidential voting choice and candidate evaluations in 2000 and 2004.[4] We re-estimated all of our models using two specifications to see whether the effectiveness of advertising depends on the characteristics of the viewer. In one specification, we interacted the individual ad exposure measures with binary variables indicating three levels of political knowledge: high, medium, and low. In the other, we interacted the individual ad exposure measures with binary variables indicating three partisan categories: Republican (weak and strong identifiers), independents (pure and leaners), and Democrats (weak and strong). In this section, we explore how variations in political information across individuals affect the impact of ad exposure on candidate evaluations and voting choice.

Following the logic laid out by Zaller (1992) and Price and Zaller (1993), we measured generalized political information in the 2000 ANES with a familiar battery of questions asking respondents to identify the "job or office" held by Supreme Court Chief Justice William Rehnquist, Senate Majority Leader Trent Lott, British Prime Minister Tony Blair, and Attorney-General Janet Reno, along with questions about partisan control of the House and Senate. A total of six questions were used to construct this knowledge scale.[5] The mean number of correct answers was 2.1. A quarter of respondents answered none of the questions correctly, and fewer than 4 percent got all six answers correct.

---

[4] As with Chapter 5, we restrict the analysis in this chapter to the general election.

[5] In a report for the American National Election Studies in March 2008, Jon Krosnick and Arthur Lupia reported on a potential coding problem in the knowledge scale questions. These problems were predominately with the 2004 ANES (a survey that we do not employ in this book) and involved the way coders assessed correct and incorrect responses. Specifically, if a respondent reported that Tony Blair was the "head of England," it was possible that this would be coded as incorrect. This, of course, might legitimately be ruled incorrect—Blair was the prime minister, and the queen is technically the head of state. However, the respondent clearly had knowledge about Tony Blair, and a more permissive criterion would record this as such. All told, it is possible, then, that low-information respondents are actually more knowledgeable than they seem.

We defined low information as those respondents who could answer a maximum of two out of six questions; this accounted for 58 percent of all respondents. Medium-information respondents were those who could answer three or four questions correctly, accounting for 32 percent of all respondents. High-information citizens were the 10 percent of respondents who answered five or all six of the questions correctly.[6]

Our measure of political information in the 2004 BYU–UW study was constructed similarly, except respondents were asked to identify the job or office held by Senate Majority Leader Bill Frist instead of Trent Lott and Attorney-General John Ashcroft instead of Janet Reno. Unlike the 2000 ANES, this study did not inquire about partisan control of each house of Congress. The average number of correct responses to the knowledge questions in this study was 1.4. In this study, 59 percent of respondents were classified as low information because they correctly answered zero or one of the four knowledge questions. Thirty-two percent of respondents were classified as medium information because they answered two or three questions correctly. And 9 percent of respondents answered all four questions correctly, earning them the high-information designation.[7]

Table 6.1 shows the results from all fourteen models. Some of the models are from 2000 and some are from 2004; some of the models concern presidential candidates and some concern U.S. Senate races. Finally, some of the models predict voting choice; others predict candidate evaluations. As with the previous two empirical chapters, despite a full battery of model controls, we report only the model estimates associated with advertising exposure.[8]

---

[6] As might be expected, if we define low, medium, and high information differently, the results change slightly. However, even with a more generous definition of high information, for example, our substantive conclusions about the type of respondent affected by exposure to political advertising do not change.

[7] Political information is not the same as level of education, although the two are positively correlated with each other at 0.46 in the 2000 ANES. Some people may be highly educated and yet have little or no knowledge of politics, while some people with little formal education may follow politics closely and know the ins and outs of the latest political news.

[8] We did not include generalized political information as a control variable in the models reported here, chiefly because we have no reason to expect levels of political knowledge to be related in any significant way to voting choice and candidate evaluations. However, if we do include such a measure in our models, the substantive results are not affected.

TABLE 6.1 Effects of Advertising Exposure on Voting Choice and Candidate Evaluations by Political Information

	Democratic exposure			Republican exposure		
	Low	Medium	High	Low	Medium	High
2000 Senate						
Vote Democrat	**0.159**	0.148	−0.140	**−0.272**	**−0.221**	0.057
	(1.72)	(1.34)	(−0.81)	**(−2.84)**	**(−1.83)**	(0.33)
Dem feeling	0.514	0.669	−0.324	−0.722	−0.881	−0.929
thermometer	(0.93)	(0.97)	(−0.37)	(−1.19)	(−1.21)	(−1.18)
Rep feeling	−0.098	−0.067	1.47	**0.966**	0.657	−1.68
thermometer	(−0.14)	(−0.07)	(1.3)	**(1.63)**	(0.71)	(−1.56)
2004 Senate						
Vote Democrat	**0.331**	0.039	0.286	**−0.267**	0.015	−0.233
	(2.78)	(0.25)	(1.15)	**(−3.02)**	(0.11)	(−1.1)
Dem favorability	0.009	0.008	0.025	−0.039	−0.035	−0.022
	(0.18)	(0.17)	(0.37)	(−0.89)	(−0.86)	(−0.31)
Rep favorability	−0.041	**−0.094**	0.001	**0.154**	**0.160**	**0.063**
	(−1.15)	**(−1.84)**	(0.02)	**(4.14)**	**(3.77)**	**(1.99)**
2000 President						
Vote Gore	−0.192	0.065	**0.430**	0.220	0.067	−0.207
	(−0.99)	(0.31)	**(2.02)**	(1.19)	(0.41)	(−0.98)
Gore likes	**0.082**	**0.150**	0.057	−0.064	−0.085	0.001
	(1.67)	**(2.63)**	(0.4)	(−1.34)	(−1.51)	(0.01)
Gore dislikes	0.078	0.045	−0.007	−0.035	−0.004	−0.013
	(1.53)	(0.88)	(−0.09)	(−0.7)	(−0.08)	(−0.18)
Bush likes	0.050	−0.022	0.001	−0.010	0.064	−0.004
	(0.97)	(−0.37)	(0.02)	(−0.2)	(1.07)	(−0.05)
Bush dislikes	0.058	**0.154**	**0.312**	−0.002	−0.094	**−0.268**
	(1.23)	**(2.54)**	**(3.46)**	(−0.05)	(−1.51)	**(−2.86)**
2004 President						
Vote Kerry	**0.353**	0.108	**0.692**	**−0.532**	−0.314	**−0.850**
	(1.63)	(0.31)	**(2.3)**	**(−2.25)**	(−0.81)	**(−2.94)**
Kerry favorability	**0.164**	0.048	0.028	**−0.176**	−0.048	−0.049
	(2.76)	(0.69)	(0.22)	**(−2.77)**	(−0.62)	(−0.38)
Bush favorability	−0.100	−0.007	0.143	0.123	0.021	−0.154
	(−1.19)	(−0.06)	(1.09)	(1.46)	(0.17)	(−1.13)

Note: Entries are coefficients and *z*-scores (in parentheses), and each row represents one model. Bold-face indicates that the variable is statistically significant at the .10 level. Voting-choice models are estimated using logit. Favorability models in 2000 (feeling thermometer) are estimated using ordinary least squares regression, while favorability models in 2004 are estimated using ordered probit. Likes and dislikes models are estimated using a generalized linear model. Control variables are not shown.

All told, the results demonstrate that the effects of advertising are widespread. Advertising matters not only for those who have moderate or high levels of political information but for low-information voters, as well. There are a couple of ways to interpret the findings. One is by examining for which group the ad exposure coefficient is highest. A higher coefficient indicates that advertising is having more of an impact on voting choice or candidate evaluations. In eleven instances, the coefficient is highest among those with low information, and in eleven instances, it is highest among those who are high in political information. In six instances, the largest coefficient is found among those with moderate levels of political information. Clearly, by this standard advertising effects are widespread—even more widespread than we had expected with our information hypothesis.

The other approach is to look at statistical significance—that is, whether the relationship between ad exposure and voting choice or candidate evaluations could have happened by chance. If one examines those coefficients that are statistically significant (the boldfaced entries in Table 6.1), the effects of ad exposure appear to be rooted disproportionately among those who are low in political information. Of the twenty-three statistically significant coefficients, eleven are found among low-information respondents; five are located in medium-information respondents; and six are for those who are high in information. This evidence supports the information hypothesis.

More specifically, in the four voting-choice specifications, advertising influenced low-information respondents in three: in their Senate voting choice in both 2000 and 2004 and in their presidential voting choice in 2004. Medium-information voters were influenced only in the 2000 Senate model (and only then for exposure to Republican ads). Ads influenced high-information respondents in both the 2000 and 2004 presidential contests but in neither of the Senate models.

As for candidate evaluations, ads had an influence on low-information respondents in the Republican Senate models in 2000, the Republican Senate favorability model in 2004, the Gore likes model in 2000, and the Kerry favorability model in 2004. Medium-information respondents were significantly affected in the Republican Senate favorability model in 2004 and in the models predicting Gore likes and Bush dislikes in the 2000 presidential contest. Among high-information respondents, ads influenced favorability toward Republican Senators in 2004 and affected the number of Bush dislikes in the 2000 presidential contest.

Notably, the evidence also suggests that exposure to Democrats' and Republicans' advertising had similar effects. Of the eleven statistically significant effects for low-information respondents, exposure to Democrats' ads was responsible for five, and exposure to Republicans ads accounted for six. Three of the five medium-information effects were from exposure to Democrats' ads, as were three of the six high-information effects.

In sum, the effects of advertising are widespread across levels of political knowledge, but to the extent that advertising influences one group more than another, it is those who are low in political information who are more likely to be persuaded.

To evaluate these ad effects in more depth, we estimated changes in the predicted probability of voting for the Democratic candidate associated with different levels of advertising exposure in the voting-choice models. We estimated these changes for a thirty-year-old, single white woman. This hypothetical respondent takes on the mean of all of the remaining control variables and is self-defined as a political independent. We vary her level of exposure to Democrats' and Republicans' ads from one-half standard deviation below the mean to one-half standard deviation above, holding exposure to the other party's ads constant. These simulated probabilities allow us to assess the effect on candidate support of moving from a modest disadvantage in the information environment to a modest advantage. We also vary her level of generalized political information. These changes in probabilities are shown in Figure 6.1.

In Senate voting in both years, advertising had its greatest impact among those who were low in political information, and this was true regardless of whether the ads came from Republicans or Democrats. When we assume that our hypothetical respondent is low in information, her probability of voting for the Democratic candidate increases by 0.14 for 2000 and by 0.22 for 2004 with increased exposure to the Democrat's ad. That probability of voting for the Democrat sensibly declines by 0.19 for 2000 and by 0.18 for 2004 with increased exposure to the Republican's ad. But if we assume the hypothetical voter has

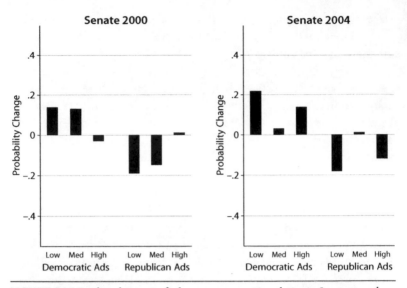

FIGURE 6.1 Predicted impact of ad exposure on voting choice in Senate races by political information

Note: The bars show the change in probability of voting for the Democratic candidate, varying exposure to ads by one standard deviation, for respondents at low, medium and high levels of political information. Med, medium.

moderate or high levels of ad exposure, the equivalent changes in probability are all smaller, nearing zero in some cases.

The story is a little different when we look at the effects of advertising on voting in a presidential election (Figure 6.2). In three of four instances here, the largest effects of changes in ad exposure are found among those who have the highest levels of political information. The change in the probability of voting for the Democrat among low-information viewers, though, given a change in ad exposure rivals the changes seen for high-information people in 2004. For instance, assuming our respondent is low in political information, her probability of voting for Kerry in 2004 declines by 0.36 when her exposure to Republicans' advertising is high. The equivalent change when we assume she is high in information is 0.40.

Up to this point, we have shown that the effects of advertising are confined not only to those with moderate or high levels of political information; rather, advertising has the capacity to persuade those

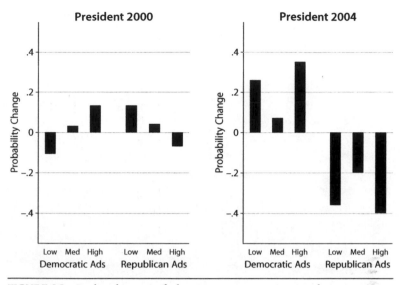

FIGURE 6.2 Predicted impact of advertising exposure on voting choice in presidential races by political information

Note: The bars show the change in probability of voting for the Democratic candidate, varying exposure to ads by one standard deviation, for respondents at low, medium, and high levels of political information. Med, medium.

with low levels of information, as well. And importantly, advertising influences low-information individuals both in very intense presidential races and less intense (at least on average) U.S. Senate races. In fact, six of the eleven statistically significant ad effects shown in Table 6.1 are located in Senate races. This suggests that advertising matters not just because of the number of messages that are being sent but also because of the nature of the messages.

At the risk of going too far afield, we suggest that understanding the unique packaging of political ads may be especially important in today's political world because the thirty-second ad looks much different than it did fifty years ago. For example, presidential ads are significantly shorter today than they were in the past, as Geer (2006) has noted. In 1960, there were more sixty-second than thirty-second ads. (Using Geer's data, forty-nine ads were fifty-five seconds or longer, compared with twenty-six ads of thirty seconds or less.) This was largely true until 1980, when thirty-second spots became more abundant. (In that year, ninety-two ads in Geer's sample were thirty seconds long, and forty-nine were sixty seconds long.) In 1996, Geer found only one sixty-second ad in his sample.[9]

Indeed, we live in a world where images and messages come at us more quickly and where citizens have ever shorter attention spans. This is often lamented, and little good is associated with the change. At the very least, however, and as the results in this section make clear, this change in the realm of political advertising has not eliminated its persuasive effect. We are cautious about this claim, but it is certainly possible that as ads have gotten shorter and quicker, their ability to persuade the least informed citizens may have been enhanced. We take this issue up again in the concluding section of the chapter, where we explore the implications a bit more deeply.

The Moderating Effect of Partisanship

We have discussed the moderating influence of political knowledge on the effectiveness of political advertising, but voters also encounter politics as Republicans, Democrats, and independents. Here, too, the effects of political advertising should work through these predispositions.[10] According to our expectations, political independents should be significantly influenced by exposure to both Republicans' and Democrats' ads. They enter campaigns with fewer attachments and might therefore be willing to listen to—and not automatically reject— arguments from both sides. We also expect Democrats and Republicans to be influenced by exposure to ads aired by their own party. As such, Democrats should not be significantly moved by exposure to Republican-sponsored ads, and similarly, Democrats' advertising should not have much impact on Republicans. In other words, we

---

[9] Only in 1992 did the sixty-second ad make a brief resurgence: twenty-one of the sixty-two ads in Geer's (2006) sample were one minute long. But this was due almost entirely to Ross Perot's advertising campaign. The number of sixty-second ads in 1984 was eleven, and in 1988, it was eight.

[10] Perhaps it would be ideal to consider the moderating influence of partisanship *and* knowledge. In other words, are low-information Democrats more affected by advertising than high-information Republicans? Such a test, while ideal, is beyond the scope of this analysis. We simply do not have enough respondents in any specific survey to sort the respondents into these finer categories.

expect partisans to be discriminating in the ads to which they pay attention and independents to be equal-opportunity listeners.

To assess these expectations, we split respondents into three categories: Democrats, Republicans, and independents. The standard survey instrument for assessing respondents' party identification is based on a series of branching questions. For example, respondents were asked first: "Generally speaking, do you think of yourself as a Republican, a Democrat, an independent, or what?" Respondents who picked the Republican Party or the Democratic Party were then asked: "Would you call yourself a strong Democrat/Republican or a not-very-strong Democrat/Republican?" An argument could be made for distinguishing between strong and not-very-strong partisans, but we chose to combine these identifiers in each party into one category so that each of our categories would have a fairly equal number of respondents.[11]

Respondents who chose to label themselves independents in the initial question were then asked, "Do you think of yourself as closer to the Republican Party or to the Democratic Party?" Regardless of their answer here, we treated them as independents in the analyses that follow.

The results from our models are reported in Table 6.2. In general, we find ad exposure effects that are more widespread than predicted. Of the eighty-four coefficient estimates in all fourteen models, thirty are significant predictors at the 0.10 level. In other words, we are fairly certain there is a true relationship between a person's partisanship and the effectiveness of advertising. Nineteen of the thirty significant coefficients were in line with the predictions of the theory. That is, ad exposure influenced independents or ad exposure influenced partisans of the ad's sponsor. But in eleven instances, partisans were swayed by advertising from the opposing party's candidate.

Beginning with the results in accord with our expectations, we found that independents were affected by exposure to Democrats' and Republicans' ads in the 2004 presidential race (for voting choice and Kerry favorability) and by exposure to Democrats' ads in the 2000

---

[11] We did, however, re-estimate all models with these five finer partisan categories: weak Democrats, strong Democrats, weak Republicans, strong Republicans, and independents. By and large, the results are substantively the same under this specification. For ease of interpretation, we talk only about the Democratic, Republican, and independent models.

TABLE 6.2 Effects of Advertising Exposure on Voting Choice and Candidate Evaluations by Partisanship

	Democratic exposure			Republican exposure		
	Dem	Ind	Rep	Dem	Ind	Rep
2000 Senate						
Vote Democrat	0.175	−0.004	0.163	−0.278	−0.109	−0.139
	(0.99)	(−0.04)	(1.2)	(−1.37)	(−0.9)	(−0.91)
Dem feeling	**1.63**	0.527	−0.176	**−1.67**	−0.608	−0.925
thermometer	**(2.18)**	(0.64)	(−0.16)	**(−2.08)**	(−0.74)	(−0.91)
Rep feeling	0.586	0.740	**−1.35**	−0.683	0.603	**1.50**
thermometer	(0.65)	(0.78)	**(−1.9)**	(−0.68)	(0.6)	**(2.35)**
2004 Senate						
Vote Democrat	**0.569**	−0.037	**0.351**	**−1.32**	−0.074	−0.105
	(3.59)	(−0.21)	**(2.16)**	**(−2.16)**	(−0.4)	(−0.84)
Dem favorability	**0.157**	0.012	−0.059	−0.048	0.000	−0.025
	(2.12)	(0.25)	(−0.85)	(−1.03)	(0)	(−0.38)
Rep favorability	−0.056	−0.033	−0.064	**0.154**	**0.113**	**0.130**
	(−1.06)	(−0.62)	(−1.12)	**(3.77)**	**(1.88)**	**(2.41)**
2000 President						
Vote Gore	−0.092	−0.022	0.156	0.130	0.135	−0.155
	(−0.49)	(−0.11)	(0.7)	(0.69)	(0.68)	(−0.75)
Gore likes	0.032	**0.123**	**0.326**	0.006	−0.088	**−0.267**
	(0.59)	**(2.05)**	**(3.47)**	(0.11)	(−1.53)	**(−2.96)**
Gore dislikes	**0.214**	0.017	0.056	**−0.170**	0.016	−0.018
	(2.18)	(0.35)	(1.01)	**(−1.66)**	(0.34)	(−0.34)
Bush likes	0.057	−0.034	0.064	−0.014	0.066	−0.026
	(0.56)	(−0.65)	(1.12)	(−0.13)	(1.32)	(−0.45)
Bush dislikes	**0.108**	**0.090**	**0.236**	−0.065	−0.006	**−0.209**
	(1.98)	**(1.63)**	**(2.37)**	(−1.17)	(−0.12)	**(−2.08)**
2004 President						
Vote Kerry	−0.019	**0.571**	**0.580**	−0.302	**−0.774**	**−0.701**
	(−0.08)	**(2.11)**	**(1.96)**	(−1.39)	**(−3.02)**	**(−2.08)**
Kerry favorability	**0.218**	**0.197**	0.053	**−0.221**	**−0.176**	−0.078
	(1.91)	**(2.67)**	(0.81)	**(−1.9)**	**(−2.47)**	(−1.05)
Bush favorability	−0.033	0.017	**−0.139**	0.075	−0.031	**0.154**
	(−0.3)	(0.2)	**(−1.72)**	(0.65)	(−0.37)	**(1.98)**

Note: Entries are coefficients and z-scores (in parentheses), and each row represents one model. Vote choice models are estimated using logit. Boldface indicates that the variable is statistically significant at the .10 level. Favorability models in 2000 (feeling thermometer) are estimated using ordinary least squares regression, while favorability models in 2004 are estimated using ordered probit. Likes and dislikes models are estimated using a generalized linear model. Control variables are not shown.

presidential election (for Gore likes and Bush dislikes). Independents exposed to large numbers of pro-Kerry ads in 2004 were more likely to vote for him and evaluated him more favorably. Exposure to pro-Gore ads in 2000 raised the number of positive assessments that independents offered about Gore and boosted negative assessments of Bush among independents. Pro-Bush advertising reached only independents in 2004, lowering the reported likelihood of voting for Kerry and lowering Kerry's favorability. In spite of the relatively abundant ad effects in the presidential race, advertising influenced independents only once in a Senate race: independents in 2004 were more likely to view Senate Republican candidates favorably under conditions of high exposure.

Exposure to Democrats' ads had an impact on Democratic partisans in at least one instance in all four races. Increased exposure to Democrats' ads raised people's evaluations of Senate Democrats in 2000 and 2004, and it boosted the likelihood of voting for the Democrat in 2004. Increased exposure to pro-Gore ads in 2000 raised reported Bush negatives among Democrats, but it also raised Gore's negatives, as well—the latter being a rare instance of a backlash effect. Finally, Democrats responded with higher Kerry favorability scores in 2004 when their exposure to pro-Kerry ads increased.

Similarly, ad exposure affected Republicans in multiple contexts. Republicans exposed to more Republicans' ads were more favorable toward Republican Senate candidates in 2000 and 2004. Pro-Bush ads in 2000 reduced the number of reported Gore likes among Republicans and lowered Bush dislikes. Finally, Republicans responded to pro-Bush ads in 2004 with a greater likelihood of voting for him and higher favorability scores.

As noted earlier, however, there were also a number of times in which partisans were influenced by ads from the opposing party, which is contrary to our expectations. These can be seen in the third and fourth columns of results in Table 6.2. For example, Republicans were influenced by Democrats' ads in the 2004 Senate voting-choice model, with more exposure leading to a higher likelihood of voting for the Democratic candidate. When Republicans were exposed to Democrats' advertising in the 2000 Senate races, their evaluations of Senate Republican candidates declined. In the 2000 presidential race, increased ad exposure to pro-Gore ads led Republicans to report a higher number of Gore likes and Bush dislikes. And in the 2004 presidential contest, Republicans were more likely to vote for Kerry and less likely to evaluate Bush favorably as their exposure to pro-Kerry ads increased.

Republicans' ads also influenced Democrats in five instances. Increased exposure to Republicans' ads lowered favorability scores for Democratic Senate candidates in 2000 and raised favorability scores for Republican Senate candidates in 2004. Democrats were also less likely to vote for Democratic Senate candidates in 2004 after being exposed to higher levels of Republicans' ads. Exposure to Republicans' ads *did* lower Gore's negatives in 2000 (a second instance in which exposure worked against the sponsor), but pro-Bush ads in 2004 lowered Kerry's favorability among Democrats.

To illustrate the substantive impact of such cross-partisan persuasion, we focus again on our hypothetical respondent, the thirty-year-old woman. We predict, under a variety of scenarios, the probability that she will vote for the Democratic candidate in both the 2004 U.S. Senate and presidential races. We vary three things in these scenarios: her level of exposure to Democrats' and Republicans' advertising, her partisanship, and her pre-election voting intention. As in the previous section, we hold all of the other variables constant. The results are reported in Table 6.3.

The simulated changes in the probability of voting for the Democratic candidate reveal the importance of the individual's party identification in moderating voting choice. For example, note the third and fourth columns of probabilities, where the cross-partisan persuasive effects are situated. When our hypothetical respondent was a Republican, exposure to Democrats' advertising had an influence on voting choice only when she had no reported pre-election voting intention (boosting her probability of voting Democratic by 0.09 in the Senate case and by 0.17 in the presidential case) or when her pre-election preference was for a Democratic candidate. The change in probability was 0.20 in the Senate case and 0.39 in the presidential context. When our hypothetical respondent reports a pre-election preference for the Republican candidate, however, Democratic advertising has no significant impact on her voting choice. The same is true when she is a Democrat initially supporting a Democrat; Republican advertising has no discernible impact on her voting choice.

TABLE 6.3 Predicted Impact of Advertising Exposure on Voting for Democratic Candidate

	Democratic exposure			Republican exposure		
	Dem	Ind	Rep	Dem	Ind	Rep
2004 Senate						
Pre-election Dem preference	0.00	−0.01	**0.20**	0.00	−0.02	−0.07
Pre-election Rep preference	**0.03**	−0.01	0.02	**−0.10**	−0.03	−0.01
No pre-election preference	0.01	−0.02	**0.09**	−0.02	−0.04	−0.03
2004 President						
Pre-election Dem preference	0.00	**0.14**	**0.39**	−0.02	**−0.18**	**−0.43**
Pre-election Rep preference	−0.01	**0.26**	0.04	**−0.19**	**−0.34**	−0.05
No pre-election preference	0.00	**0.33**	**0.17**	−0.07	**−0.42**	**−0.20**

Note: Entries are changes in probabilities of voting for the Democratic candidate under conditions of varied Democratic or Republican exposure, which is varied by one standard deviation. Results are from models reported in Table 6.2. Boldfaced entries are either noted in the text or are statistically significant at the .10 level.

At the same time, advertising serves to bring home those who have wandered from supporting their party's candidate. For example, when our hypothetical respondent is a Republican who reports a pre-election voting preference for Kerry, exposure to pro-Bush ads increased the likelihood she would vote for Bush. Increasing her exposure to pro-Bush ads boosted the probability she would vote for him by 0.43.

As a whole, our results provide limited evidence for the partisanship hypothesis. We had expected to find stronger and more consistent effects of advertising on independent voters (who *did* respond quite strongly to advertising in the 2004 presidential case, as Table 6.3 demonstrates) and almost no effects of opposite party advertising on partisans. What we found, though, was that partisans were often influenced by advertising—even advertising from the opposite party. This is encouraging from a normative perspective. Persuasion appears to be widespread among partisan subgroups, often drawing in those with some hesitation about their preferred party's candidate. We cannot be sure why exactly these Democrats or Republicans were initially hesitant to commit to their party's candidate (in their pre-election interview), but ads speak principally to these partisans, working to accelerate that defection or to prevent it.

Discussion

In the end, we find that the influence of advertising is moderated most consistently through political knowledge, with those who are lower in political information more influenced by ads' messages. That said, we have shown evidence that ads can persuade regardless of the individual's level of political awareness. These findings point to an important distinction in the way types of political information influence citizens. If political information disseminated through more difficult-to-process channels (such as television news reports and print media) influences only the politically knowledgeable (as other research has suggested), but political ads are able to influence most everyone, then there is an important gap in the information resources available to voters.

The implications of the gap depend in part on differences (content, tone, etc.) between advertising and these other sources, but the gap's presence is certainly worthy of more study. This may be even more true as information disseminates to citizens in ever changing ways. For example, some argue that the thirty-second television ad will soon be replaced by micro-targeting through the Internet. We are not so convinced of the immediacy of such a change, but if it happens, those with lower levels of political information may be less susceptible to influence because Internet messages can be longer, more detailed, and more nuanced—and thus less likely to be comprehended by those who are low in political awareness.

Like print media, blog posts and political e-mails require at least a modest level of background information to understand. Such messages also very rarely come to voters uninvited, as television ads do. If campaigns abandon television as a method of campaigning, those with lower levels of political awareness are likely—all else being equal—to rely less on campaign information when making decisions, and more on their political predispositions, such as their party attachments and economic considerations. Whether this is good or bad for voters' decision making is arguable, but it is certainly something that campaign managers who want to change minds are likely to lament.

In terms of the moderating influence of partisanship, we do not find that the effect of advertising was greatest among political independents. Rather, the effects were—to use our favorite word again—

widespread. This is certainly unexpected, but it also suggests some-thing important about American politics. Notably, exposure to advertising is not as polarizing as one might expect. If Democrats only listened to Democrats and Republicans only listened to Republicans, television ads would have the effect of simply reinforcing predisposi-tions. Indeed, this is what we generally thought we would find. With these results, however, we can more confidently assert that ads *do* have some persuasive power—even among those who might not initially be inclined to support a candidate.

Of course, we must also caution that cross-partisan effects are not generally driving people away from their predispositions. Republi-cans, for example, are still overwhelmingly expected to vote for the Republican candidates and view Republicans more favorably (at least, compared with Democrats and independents), and this is true regard-less of levels of advertising exposure. The results only indicate that, all else being equal, Republicans and Democrats are not deaf to the other side.

Indeed, this finding is consistent with some recent scholarship that shows the effectiveness of cross-partisan appeals through the use of so-called wedge issues—such as immigration, gay marriage, and abortion—which serve to divide supporters of one political party. When the other party's candidate campaigns on such issues and makes them important in the minds of voters, it can actually persuade them to vote for the candidate from the other party (Hillygus and Shields 2009). One example that Hillygus and Shields give of the effective use of a wedge issue comes from 2004, when Democrats campaigned in favor of embryonic stem-cell research, an issue that divided Republican vot-ers. Perhaps, then, we should not be so surprised that advertising can influence even those with attachments to the other political party.

But what about the argument that ads are manipulating low-information voters into casting ballots for candidates who may not represent their best interests? Ultimately, of course, we cannot say with certainty that ads are *not* manipulating (we could never know this without more in-depth interviews of the respondents), but the results relative to the partisanship hypothesis are reassuring. Because cross-partisan exposure effects are principally limited to those with a pre-existing preference for the other candidate or no candidate, persuasion here is not often changing low-information Republican voters into Democratic supporters or low-information Democratic voters into Republican supporters. It is most often nudging these partisans toward the candidate they already support, even if that candidate does not match their partisan identification, or it is bringing partisans back "home" to their own party (Table 6.3). In this sense, then, there is very little evidence here that ads are working to trick people into supporting candidates whom they normally would disapprove of or dislike.

With these results, we have almost concluded our empirical investigation of the persuasive force of paid political advertising. In showing that ads have disproportionately more impact in open-seat races and in competitive races (Chapter 4); that fear and anger appeals can work both for and against a candidate (Chapter 5); and that ads influence many types of voters (this chapter), we have advanced theoretical and empirical understandings of the role of political advertising in contemporary American elections. Persuasion happens, and it happens often. In this chapter alone, the evidence indicates that television may be one way for the less aware to hear and respond to candidates and for cross-partisan influence to break through the blue–red divide that we hear so much about these days.

There is, however, one other way by which televised political advertising might influence the choices that people make at the ballot box. Advertising can have an influence on viewers not only through the direct impact of paid ads, but also through the news media or on the Internet. We demonstrate in the next chapter that there is substantial discussion of political advertising by the news media in recent elections and that exposure to political ad messages has grown dramatically on the Internet in the past decade.

7 How Ad Coverage in News Matters

I T IS A WELL-KNOWN STORY, at least to those who study political advertising: in 1964, President Lyndon Johnson's campaign created and aired the infamous "Daisy Girl" ad. It featured a young girl who was plucking petals off a flower while in the background an ominous voice counted down as if preparing for a missile launch. When the count reached zero, an explosion appeared in the background, giving the effect that a nuclear bomb had been detonated. Because of the fury the ad caused, Johnson's campaign pulled it after it had aired only once. But virtually the whole country knew something about it, as it was aired on national news broadcasts and became the center of national conversation.

Such ads—those whose impact is amplified by the news media—are not all that rare. The Willie Horton ad from the presidential campaign in 1988 comes to mind; the ad accused the Democratic candidate Michael Dukakis of giving weekend prison passes to first-degree murderers. The Swift Boat Veterans ads aired in 2004 are another good example. In this final empirical chapter, we take up two recent developments in political advertising: the amplification of political ads through media coverage—a trend that is on the rise—and the growth of advertising designed for or disseminated through the Internet. While our research has considered seriously the effects of exposure to televised political advertising on voting choice, there are increasingly greater opportunities for voters—even those without televisions—to encounter campaign spots elsewhere, and these opportunities deserve some discussion.

Media Coverage of Ads

Consider first an example of an ad covered aggressively by the news media during the 2006 elections. The ad, paid for by the National Republican Senatorial Committee (NRSC) and aired in the waning weeks of the 2006 U.S. Senate contest in Tennessee, was one of the most memorable of that year. A *Washington Post* writer called it "one of the funniest, slickest, best-produced political ads of the year." The *Post* writer described the ad, which was aired against the Democrat Harold Ford Jr., this way:

> A succession of stupid or shady characters expresses support for Ford, applauding him because he wants to make families pay higher taxes or take guns away from hunters. A greasy guy in dark sunglasses claims Ford has taken contributions from pornographers, but shrugs and adds, "Who hasn't?" Among the mock endorsers is a blond bimbo—sorry, but that's the only word—who squeals, "I met Harold at the Play-boy party!" At the end of the ad she reappears, suggesting a certain intimacy as she implores, "Harold, call me."

Critics of the ad were numerous. Among the complaints was that the ad was sending not-so-subtle racially charged messages, given that Ford is African American and the "bimbo" was white. Some believed the ad was trying to play on whites' fears of interracial dating. John Geer, a political scientist, was quoted in the *New York Times* as saying the ad "makes the Willie Horton ad look like child's play." Even Ford's opponent in the race, the Republican Bob Corker, called on the NRSC to take down the ad.

Data on how many times this ad aired in Tennessee, or how much the Republican Party paid to air the ad, are hard to come by, as our main sources of ad-tracking data, the Wisconsin Advertising Project, was active in only five Midwestern states in 2006. But we do know that a lot of Tennesseans—and people from others states, as well—knew about the ad. A Mason–Dixon poll of Tennessee residents conducted a few days after the ad went off the air found that 81 percent of them had seen it. The big question for us, however, is how that exposure to the ad occurred. Undoubtedly, many Tennesseans saw the ad during a commercial break on their local television station, but how many of them also—or solely—saw the ad featured on a news broadcast, saw it on the Internet, heard about it on the radio, or read about it in a newspaper? Until now, we have assessed the influence of ads only in the first case: exposure on television during a commercial break.

Certainly, there was ample opportunity to learn about the ad. Both the national ABC and CBS nightly news broadcasts aired a story about it, and NBC aired three between the time the ad was first aired on October 20 and Election Day.[1] National newspapers also weighed in on the controversial ad. The *Washington Post* printed six articles that mentioned the ad between when it was first aired and Election Day, and the *New York Times* contributed six articles.[2] The Associated Press distributed another sixteen articles that made mention of the ad during the same time period.

Local media also got into the act. The *Chattanooga Times and Free Press* mentioned the ad in eight stories between October 21 and November 5 and printed three opinion pieces, all of which inveighed against what the writers saw as a dirty ad. The ad also rapidly made its way onto YouTube. As of mid-2008, the ad had been viewed on that website about 400,000 times. YouTube, of course, is only one of the many websites on which people may have seen the ad.

In sum, even if Tennessee voters did not happen to catch an airing of the ad that was paid for by the NRSC, they still would have had ample opportunity to become familiar with it. But what is the impact of these additional opportunities to be exposed to advertising?

In this chapter, we will first establish that the potentially persuasive effects of advertising, beyond the original ad airings, has been growing over the past couple of decades. Moreover, we will argue that

---

[1] Data on the network-news discussions of advertising come from the Vanderbilt Television News Archive, available online at http://tvnews.vanderbilt.edu (accessed October 27, 2010).

[2] Newspaper counts come from a search on Lexis–Nexis for "Harold w/2 Ford) AND (ad OR advert*) AND Playboy."

the persuasive impact of advertising is likely to be different depending on the medium through which one is exposed. Finally, we will turn to some statistical analysis that allows us to see whether exposure to advertising through the news media as opposed to through paid spots might affect their candidate preferences.

The news media seem more attracted to the coverage of televised political advertising these days than in the past. It is a trend that West (2008) documents by counting the number of *New York Times, CBS Evening News,* and *Washington Post* stories that have covered advertising in each presidential general election since the 1970s. According to West (2008, 70), "The general trend was a substantial increase in coverage of advertisements in the 1980s and 1990s." He does, however, note a drop in ad coverage in the 2000 and 2004 general elections.

Although West's data are suggestive, he does not account for whether there may have been a change in the total amount of coverage that was devoted to the presidential campaign more generally. To control for that possibility, we show in Table 7.1 ad-related coverage (stories that make mention of political advertising) as a *proportion* of total campaign coverage. More specifically, we show the percentage of campaign-related articles printed in September and October that mentioned political advertising by news source and year.[3] Data from the *Washington Post* and Associated Press go back to 1980, while data from the *New York Times* are available back to 1976. Clearly, our data are broadly consistent with West's claim that ad coverage has increased, both in terms of the number of articles that mention advertising and in terms of the percentage of total campaign coverage that is related to advertising.

In the *Washington Post,* for instance, one sees a large spike in the percentage of ad-related coverage in 1988, and that percentage continues to rise to the year 2000, when almost 15 percent of campaign coverage was ad-related. There is a dip in the next two election years, to 9.4 percent in 2004 and 11.6 percent in 2008, but those percentages

---

[3] Data come from a Lexis–Nexis search of all dates in September and October in each election year. We searched for articles that contained the names of either the Democratic or the Republican presidential nominee to create a baseline of campaign coverage. We then searched within these results for articles that contained the term "ad" or "advert*" to create a count of ad-related campaign coverage.

TABLE 7.1 Campaign Ad–Related Stories Appearing in Major News Sources in September and October of Presidential Election Years

	Year	Ad-related articles	Campaign articles	Ad-related percentage
Washington Post	1980	56	1,512	3.7
	1984	55	1,880	2.9
	1988	78	1,010	7.7
	1992	140	1,594	8.8
	1996	145	1,696	8.5
	2000	151	1,029	14.7
	2004	179	1,896	9.4
	2008	156	1,343	11.6
Associated Press	1980	50	3,653	1.4
	1984	54	4,034	1.3
	1988	175	2,458	7.1
	1992	157	2,134	7.4
	1996	233	3,472	6.7
	2000	263	2,205	11.9
	2004	299	3,662	8.2
	2008	240	2,161	11.1
New York Times	1976	23	1,022	2.3
	1980	54	2,366	2.3
	1984	24	2,324	1.0
	1988	35	1,027	3.4
	1992	102	1,830	5.6
	1996	68	1,860	3.7
	2000	100	1,427	7.0
	2004	75	2,215	3.4
	2008	76	1,373	5.5

are still the third- and second-highest, respectively, of any year in our analysis of the *Post*.

A very similar trend is noted in Associated Press ad-related coverage, which jumps considerably from 1984 to 1988 and reaches a peak in 2000 before declining a bit in 2004 and bouncing back in 2008. Again, however, the third-highest percentage of ad coverage was in 2004, and the second-highest percentage was in 2008. The percentage of ad-related coverage in the *New York Times* is a bit lower than in the *Post* and Associated Press, yet it still follows a similar pattern, with a jump in 1988 and a peak in 2000.

TABLE 7.2 Distribution of Senate Ad-Related and Ad-Focused Articles by Newspaper in 2004

State	Newspaper	No. of campaign articles	% of ad-related articles	% of ad-focused articles
Colorado	*Denver Post*	137	15.3	11.7
Florida	*St. Petersburg Times*	83	27.7	18.1
Georgia	*Atlanta Journal-Constitution*	81	11.1	6.2
Louisiana	*New Orleans Times-Picayune*	87	5.7	1.1
Missouri	*St. Louis Post Dispatch*	47	21.3	17.0
N. Carolina	*Winston-Salem Journal*	47	12.8	10.6
Oklahoma	*Tulsa World*	88	8.0	4.5
Pennsylvania	*Pittsburgh Post Gazette*	26	11.5	11.5
Washington	*Seattle Times*	47	23.4	14.9
Wisconsin	*Milwaukee Journal Sentinel*	50	16.0	6.0

Source: Reproduced from Ridout and Smith 2008.

While our data are consistent with West's in that they show an over-all increase in ad-related coverage, we do not observe as much of a decline as he does in the most recent elections. We find, in contrast, that when one controls for the total number of campaign-related articles, the peak was in 2000, with 2008 close behind. In sum, media coverage of advertising is increasing, and it is substantial, exceeding 10 percent of total campaign coverage in some news outlets in recent years.

Devoting considerable coverage to campaign advertising is done not only by the national news media or only in presidential elections. Other research focusing on U.S. Senate races has found substantial coverage of advertising by statewide newspapers, as well. Table 7.2 (reproduced from Ridout and Smith 2008) shows the percentage of total campaign articles in ten different U.S. Senate races from 2004 that are ad-related (they mention political advertising) and ad-focused (the story is almost entirely about political advertising). Ad-related stories range from about 6 percent in coverage of the Louisiana Senate race to almost 28 percent in the Florida Senate race that year.

These numbers are worth reflecting on: more than one out of every four stories about the Florida Senate race mentioned political advertising. That seems an astonishingly high number, though the fact that 18 percent of the stories printed about that race were *focused* on the candidates' advertising (the final column of Table 7.2) is perhaps even more striking. Unsurprisingly, ad-focused articles constitute a smaller share of coverage than ad-related articles, but stories that focus on advertising are still substantial, making up more than 10 percent of coverage in Colorado, Florida, Missouri, North Carolina, Pennsylvania, and Washington.

In case anyone had any doubt of the ubiquity of ad coverage, a study of advertising in gubernatorial campaigns also confirms this conclusion (Fowler and Ridout 2009). And it is not just newspapers in which this phenomenon occurs. Additional research has found ad-related coverage to be considerable on local television news broadcasts as well (Fowler and Ridout 2009). On average, about 20 percent of local television news coverage of U.S. Senate and gubernatorial campaigns in 2006 mentioned political advertising, with about 8 percent of the campaign-related stories focusing on advertising.

Why is there so much focus in the media on political advertising? One factor that might contribute to substantial coverage of political advertising is that the launching of an ad is something new and novel for the political reporter to cover, especially if that reporter has been covering the same speech for the past several weeks. Second, ads frequently contain conflict and controversy. An ad may respond to an earlier attack made by one's opponent or may itself, in a comparative ad, contrast the positions of two candidates. Coverage of advertising would appear to be a no-brainer for reporters, given the penchant of news organizations to cover conflict (Bartels 1988; Patterson and McClure 1976; Robinson and Sheehan 1983).

Finally, advertising is easy to cover. Writing a story about a new political ad does not require the reporter to do a lot of difficult research or travel to an isolated location. Rather, the reporter merely has to view the ad and rephrase what it says, perhaps gathering a quote from each campaign about its content. Making things even easier for the reporter is that campaigns promote coverage of their ads. Often, campaigns will even send out press releases announcing the unveiling of new ads. Given recent cuts in the size of newsroom staffs as economic pressures strike news organizations, and given the demand for twenty-four-hour news these days (Leighley 2004), covering something easy such as advertising makes even more sense than it did in the past.

That people are increasingly viewing paid political advertising in the free media (on news broadcasts and in newspapers) has important implications for the study of both political advertising and American democracy itself. With regard to the former, because exposure to political advertising occurs in ways beyond what political scientists and communications scholars can measure means that even the most advanced methods of measuring ad exposure are still probably underestimating the amount of advertising to which people are exposed. If this underestimation affects all kinds of people in the same way, then the failure to account for "free media" ad exposure should not be much of a concern. But it is likely that this underestimation is systematic, especially evident among high-level media users.

A second methodological issue of concern to scholars is that the mix of advertising to which people are exposed—in terms of its tone or the specific emotions elicited—may not be an accurate reflection of the mix of advertising that the candidates are airing. Evidence suggests that the news media are more likely to mention negative and contrast ads than positive ads (Fowler and Ridout 2009; Ridout and Smith 2008); thus, scholars may not be adequately capturing the true tone of the advertising to which people are exposed. As such, the conclusions of observational studies examining the influence of ad tone on voting choice (admittedly, that includes the ones in this book) may be misleading if they fail to account for exposure to ads beyond paid advertising.

And consider the normative implications of such patterns. Pundits and prognosticators spend lots of time bemoaning negativity in American political campaigns. It may very well be the news media, however, that are magnifying the problem by focusing so heavily on the most negative spots.

Beyond these considerations, ad amplification says something interesting about the relationship between the news media and candidates—and who is setting the agenda. On the one hand, the news media appear to have the upper hand in this relationship, as reporters get to choose which ads to discuss, which of the candidates' messages to amplify. Obviously, when the message disseminated is one such as "Harold Ford likes to party at the Playboy mansion" or "John Kerry lied about his heroism in Vietnam," the news media have

great potential to influence voters' perceptions of the candidates—
and, as a possible consequence, their votes. Here the media may be
powerful actors. Even when the message is positive ("Chuck Norris is
a cool guy who likes Mike Huckabee," to reference a commonly discussed ad from 2008), the minds of voters may be changed through
the media coverage.

Looked at from a different angle, though, candidates appear to
have the upper hand and are arguably "using" the news media in this
relationship. In this view, all the candidate must do is craft an interesting or controversial ad, say something negative about his or her opponent, and the news media will come flocking to repeat that negative
message to a wide audience. One good example of a candidate having
the upper hand was Howard Dean, who, in his quest for the Democratic presidential nomination in 2004, aired a combative anti-Bush
television ad about 300 times in Austin in August 2003. It seems fairly
obvious that Dean's intent was not to garner votes for Texas's Democratic primary about seven months away; rather, it was to get reporters to write articles about him poking the eye of George W. Bush,
whose ranch in Crawford, Texas, was in the range of Austin broadcast
television. That free media attention may well have been worth much
more than the estimated $100,000–$200,000 that he spent on the
Texas ad campaign (Simon 2003).

During the 2008 election, this tactic was more obvious. The col-
umnist Howard Kurtz, for example, noted that the most discussed
Obama and McCain ads in the media were the ads that candidates
aired the least often and spent the least money on. He wrote in September 2008 in the *Washington Post*: "It is an open secret by now that
both campaigns are flooding the market with what amount to video
press releases. The phantom spots receive enormous amounts of free
airtime, particularly on cable news channels, and are the subject of
news stories and 'ad watch' features in newspapers. Journalists have
no way of knowing in advance which spots will involve a substantial
buy and which will not."

The tactic allows candidates to score short-term media coverage
of their attacks on opponents while remaining fairly positive in their
more frequently aired spots. Of course, it also implicates candidates in
the problem we noted earlier, in which the media, with their appetite

for negativity, devote considerable coverage to conflict and candidates' bickering. In this sense, the campaign ad and candidates' push for free media coverage has potentially amplified and accelerated the level of negativity people see in press reports. In short, we can hardly blame the media alone for covering negative campaign ads, given that candidates are more than willing to serve them up on a silver platter.

Even if candidates—or, increasingly, unconnected groups these days—have the upper hand in these situations, this does not diminish the potential impact of people's exposure to political advertising beyond the paid ad. There is even a potential irony in all of this. It might be that because negative ads, or fear ads or anger ads, may sometimes lead to viewer backlashes, that when candidates push for free media coverage of these controversial spots, it creates even more opportunity for viewers to react with disgust and turn against the sponsor of the ad.

Although it is difficult to prove that the media coverage of an ad has ever made *the* difference in a race, we can point to some suggestive initial evidence. In polling following the "Harold, call me" ad in Tennessee, 23 percent of respondents said that they would be less likely to vote for Ford as a result of seeing the ad—signifying in this case that the ad had its intended effect.[4] Again, we cannot say for sure how many people were exposed to the ad through traditional paid media and how many were exposed through the media amplification of the ad, but it seems likely that the only exposure for some was through the media's coverage.

Estimating the Persuasive Power of Ad Coverage

Given the anecdotal case of the anti-Harold Ford ad, can we demonstrate in a more systematic fashion that exposure to all of the varying ways in which advertising is mentioned in the news media can influence the votes that people cast? To the best of our knowledge, there is

---

[4] The poll was conducted by Mason–Dixon Polling and Research of Washington, D.C., from November 1 through November 3, 2006. A sample of 625 Tennesseans who were likely to vote in the November election were interviewed by telephone. The poll's marginals were accessed online at http://www.msnbc.msn.com/id/15547024 (accessed July 3, 2008).

no existing evidence of such an effect in the current literature. In an attempt to assess the impact of ad coverage, we rely on a survey conducted during the 2006 U.S. Senate campaigns in five different Midwestern states and coding of several newspapers and local news broadcasts that covered those campaigns.

The survey data come from the University of Wisconsin–UCLA component of the 2006 Cooperative Congressional Election Study (CCES).[5] This portion of the survey had respondents from eight media markets in five states: Illinois (Springfield and Chicago), Michigan (Detroit), Minnesota (Minneapolis–St. Paul), Ohio (Cleveland and Columbus), and Wisconsin (Madison and Milwaukee). Because Illinois had no Senate race in 2006, we eliminate respondents from that state. This was a panel study, with both a pre-election wave, which took place from mid-October until right before Election Day, and a post-election wave.

The study was somewhat unique in that respondents were interviewed not over the telephone or through a mail questionnaire but over the Internet. Polimetrix, the company that conducted the survey, samples from a volunteer panel of respondents, then uses statistical matching to create a sample that looks similar to a random sample of adult consumers in the United States across a set of specified characteristics, including age, gender, and race. It is not possible to assess whether the resulting sample is representative across other (unmatched) characteristics, although some comparisons find that the resulting sample is similar in many other ways (Vavreck and Rivers 2008). That said, there are some who still urge caution when using opt-in Internet samples (Yeager et al. 2009).

---

[5] The 2006 CCES was an online survey of 38,443 respondents fielded in October and November 2006 by Polimetrix. The study was a collaboration among thirty-nine universities. A design committee worked to write the first forty questions of the survey, called the Common Content, which were given to all respondents. The Common Content was followed by different questionnaires from CCES university teams, which were asked of a subset of respondents. Respondents who completed the questionnaires were selected from the Polimetrix PollingPoint Panel using sample matching. The Common Content was matched to the 2004 American Community Study conducted by the U.S. Bureau of the Census; however, the University of Wisconsin–UCLA portion of the CCES was matched to the 2000 U.S. Census to enable sample matching by media market. For more information on the 2006 CCES, see http://projects.iq.harvard.edu/cces/home (accessed October 27, 2010). For more information on sample matching, see Rivers 2006.

Using these survey data, we developed a statistical model predicting respondents' voting choices in their state's U.S. Senate race, expressed as voting for the Democratic candidate. One key independent variable is the respondent's exposure to political advertising, measured as the difference in exposure to Democrats' and Republicans' ads. To create this ad exposure measure, we used the same procedures we have used throughout the book and again relied on Wisconsin Advertising Project data.

The other important predictor of voting choice in our model is the individual's exposure to media coverage of political advertising in the race of interest. Here we focused on both local television news broadcasts and local newspaper coverage. To create an individual-level measure of exposure to ad-related news coverage, we used data on the volume of ad-related coverage on the local television station that the respondent reported watching the most and the local newspaper or newspapers the respondent reported reading.

The television data come from the University of Wisconsin's News-Lab, whose coders characterized each campaign-related story on a variety of factors, including whether and to what extent it mentioned advertising.[6] Local newspaper information came from a database we created of newspaper ad-mentions from eleven different newspapers serving the eight media markets for which we have advertising data.[7] A graduate-student coder examined all campaign-related articles in these newspapers printed between September 7, 2006, and November 6, 2006, noting all mentions of political advertising.

To be clear, we multiplied the number of ad-related mentions (by party) in each news source by the frequency with which each respondent used that source (a proportion that ranged from 0 for "not at all" to 1 for "almost every day"). For example, if a respondent reported reading the *Milwaukee Journal Sentinel* every day, and the paper featured the Democratic Senate candidate's advertising in a large propor-

---

[6] The Midwest News Index is a project of the University of Wisconsin's NewsLab. The NewsLab monitored the highest-rated early and late-evening half-hour of news coverage aired during the sixty days before Election Day 2006 on thirty-five television stations in five Midwestern states. For more information on the NewsLab, see http://dept.polisci .wisc.edu/uwnewslab/ (accessed October 27, 2010).

[7] These eleven newspapers were the *Detroit News, Detroit Free Press, Ann Arbor News, Minneapolis Star Tribune, St. Paul Pioneer Press, Cleveland Plain Dealer, Akron Beacon-Journal, Columbus Dispatch, Wisconsin State Journal, Capital Times,* and *Milwaukee Journal Sentinel.*

tion of its campaign reports, that respondent is expected to have a high exposure to the newspaper's Democratic advertising coverage. We then summed this over all local news media that the respondent reported using. This left us with individual-level measures of exposure to local television news and local newspaper coverage of advertising for each candidate. Finally, we logged the ad coverage exposure measure to be consistent with our advertising measure.[8]

Other predictors in our model were the respondent's vote preference in the first wave of the survey; state indicator variables (Wisconsin serves as the omitted category); the respondent's level of education, age, gender, race, income, and marital status; and party identification.

Table 7.3 shows the results of a binary choice model predicting reported vote in the Senate race. Importantly, exposure to paid political advertising has an impact on voting choice—a finding consistent with the results in previous chapters on the 2000 and 2004 elections. Stated differently, as the Democratic candidate's ad exposure advantage increases (as experienced during commercial breaks), people are more likely to vote for that Democratic candidate. In fact, the predicted probability of voting for the Democratic candidate rises by 0.31 when the Democratic exposure advantage is changed from one-half standard deviation below to one-half standard deviation above the mean.[9]

Notably, however, exposure to unpaid political advertising does not have the same impact. The probability of voting for the Democratic Senate candidate is unrelated to the Democratic candidate's advantage in terms of ad coverage in newspapers and on local television news. Thus, our suspicion that ad amplification through the news media might influence voting choice is not supported by this analysis.[10]

---

[8] Instead of separate exposure measures for Democrats and Republicans, as in previous chapters, we used a partisan advantage measure for both paid ad exposure and media ad exposure to avoid straining the statistical model, given our relatively small usable sample of respondents in this survey.

[9] This is the average change across all observations. All other predictor variables are held at their original values in the dataset.

[10] Nor is it supported if we try using different measures of ad coverage exposure. We tried using unlogged measures and using separate television and newspaper measures, but neither of these changes resulted in ad coverage having a significant impact on voting choice.

TABLE 7.3 The Influence of Paid Advertising and Ad-Related Media Coverage

	Coefficient	S.E.	z-score
Prior support for Democrat	9.284	2.779	3.340
Dem ad advantage (logged)	2.385	1.217	1.960
Dem ad coverage advantage (logged)	−1.069	1.585	−0.670
Michigan	−4.417	2.456	−1.800
Minnesota	1.252	3.880	0.320
Ohio	−1.221	3.337	−0.370
Education	0.568	0.535	1.060
Age	0.079	0.075	1.060
Male	−0.298	1.641	−0.180
White	−2.298	6.116	−0.380
Income	0.274	0.252	1.090
Married	−2.479	1.919	−1.290
Party ID	−0.939	0.479	−1.960
Constant	−10.808	9.201	−1.170
N	335		
Chi-square	327.6 ($p < .001$)		

Source: Survey data come from UW–UCLA portion of the 2006 CCES.
Note: Dependent variable is a reported vote for the Democratic Senate candidate. Model estimated using logit.

That we failed to find such an effect of free media ad coverage is not a huge surprise, however. First, coverage of political advertising, while a significant portion of all campaign-related coverage, is swamped in the typical campaign by the number of paid political ads. The opportunity then for ad coverage to have a discernible (and specific) impact on voting choice is smaller. Second, our analysis assumed that all coverage was good coverage; that having one's ads discussed in the news media would have a positive impact on the likelihood of accumulating votes.

Certainly, the literature on "ad watches" (a very specific type of ad-related coverage where reporters investigate the veracity of claims made in election-related ads) suggests that this assumption is a fair one. Pfau and Louden (1994), for example, show that ad watches in television news tend to reinforce the ad's intended message to the benefit of the sponsoring candidate (see also Ansolabehere and Iyengar 1996); this is largely because the local news coverage of an ad often replays it, or a portion of it. That said, it is not immediately clear that such effects would result from other types of ad-related media coverage—or coverage in a newspaper, which lacks the visual impact of television. Finally, because our model put all coverage of advertising together in one basket, we were not able to test for the potential impact of a single prominent ad, such as a "Daisy Girl" ad or the anti-Harold Ford ad.

In sum, while our statistical test did not reveal a direct impact of ad coverage on voting choice, we are unwilling to dismiss the possibility that it might have an effect—or that coverage of certain ads at certain points in time might matter. More research on this question is surely needed. Nonetheless, the results are a bit reassuring with respect to our previous empirical chapters. It appears that even when controlling for ad-related media exposure, paid advertising exposure retains its significant persuasive effect. In other words, even though we did not include a measure of exposure to media coverage of advertising in previous chapters, our reported results likely remain unbiased.

One other possibility worth considering, however, is that political advertising as disseminated on the Internet might have an impact on the choices that voters make. We first discussed this idea in Chapter 1, and we conclude this chapter with a longer treatment of the possibility.

Political Advertising in the Internet Age

In 1996, if you did not live in Minnesota, then you probably would not have seen an ad aired in that state's U.S. Senate race—unless, of course, the ad generated so much attention that it got replayed on a national news broadcast or cable news channel. Today, people living in California or Rhode Island (or Israel or South Africa or Argentina, for that matter) have Internet access to just about every political ad ever aired. Often, candidates, political parties, and interest groups will post all of their ads on their own websites, and even if this is not the case, people commonly post particularly interesting ads on YouTube or other, similar websites within hours of their first airing. The hope is that a candidate's ad will "go viral," working to benefit the campaign at barely no cost.

According to statistics provided by YouTube, for example, 2.7 million people have watched the 2006 ad in which Michael J. Fox, the actor stricken with Parkinson's disease, speaks up for stem-cell research and urges a vote for the Missouri Democrat Claire McCaskill for U.S. Senate. Almost as impressive, 2.1 million people have viewed the ad created for Mike Huckabee's presidential nomination campaign in which Huckabee announces he will secure the border with the assistance of the action star Chuck Norris. Another Huckabee ad—his closely analyzed Christmas ad with the bookshelf "cross" in the background—received well over 1 million views on YouTube.

In very recent years, some of the most widely viewed ads online were never aired on broadcast television. For instance, the "Yes, We Can" ad—a music video, really—in which celebrities sing along to an Obama speech, was viewed by more than 8 million people in its first four months on YouTube. The video was produced and distributed independently of the Obama campaign. And more than 5 million people have watched the anti-Hillary Clinton ad that is a takeoff on an Apple Computer ad from 1984.

Although such online ads have the *potential* to persuade voters, our contention is they are likely to have less influence on the vote than ads amplified by the news media. First, the people who watch political ads online are unlikely to be as politically and demographically diverse as the people who see ads during a news broadcast or read about an ad in the newspaper. In general, the people who are most likely to make the a conscious decision to view a candidate's ad—which is what is required online—are most likely supporters of that candidate.

Obama supporters, for example, may have been interested in viewing an inspirational video about him online or an attack on McCain, but indifferent or independent voters or those who supported John McCain are unlikely to have had any interest in viewing such ads. Similarly, visitors to John McCain's 2008 presidential campaign website were probably not undecided voters seeking out information on his policy positions, but existing or likely supporters of John McCain. Maybe they were drawn there by a post on Redstate.com or Townhall.com—two large conservative political websites—or maybe a friend sent a link, or maybe they just wanted to see how they could help out the candidate they supported. Regardless, most visitors to McCain's website were likely reliably to the right of center.

This audience stands in stark contrast to the audience for McCain or Obama ads that appeared during the local news at 6 P.M., which reached people who ranged the political spectrum, from the most ardent liberals to the most vehement conservatives, with lots of independent and undecided voters in between. Moreover, these people did not need to search for a political website or click somewhere to be exposed to an advertisement. The potential for passive learning (Zukin and Snyder 1984)—for ads to have an influence even though the recipient is not actively engaged—still exists on television. Online ads, in contrast, may do a better job of increasing the enthusiasm of supporters than of convincing people to vote for one candidate instead of another.

There is almost no scholarly research that tests the assumption that online ads disproportionately reach a candidate's core supporters, but we can offer some suggestive evidence here. We collected a series of data from Experian Hitwise, an online intelligence service that tracks web traffic to top sites. Hitwise provided to us a metric of web traffic to Obama's and McCain's sites in the fall of 2008 for all 210 media markets in the United States. We were curious whether Obama's (and McCain's) web traffic was higher in places that were predisposed to vote for him. If this is the case, then it suggests that those who visit websites are largely the converted, not the persuadable.

Figure 7.1 shows the predicted relationship between Kerry's percentage of the vote in a particular media market in 2004—our proxy for how Obama-friendly people living in a media market are—and Hitwise's ratio of Obama versus McCain website visits.[11] The y-axis is a metric that allows for comparison with overall web visits nationally. A market scoring above 100 is one in which a disproportionately larger percentage of residents are visiting the site compared with the national average. For McCain, web visits are highest in the markets where Bush performed well in 2004. Obama sees below-average traffic from these deep-red media markets and disproportionately greater visits from deep-blue markets. The slope of the McCain line is steeper

---

[11] The line was generated from a model predicting web traffic at the market level that includes a number of control variables. These include the median income of the market; turnout in 2004; the percentage of residents who identified as white, black, Hispanic, and Asian; the percentage of the market with residents who were older than sixty-five and younger than twenty-five; and the percentage of the market lying in a Southern state. The models also include a dummy variable for whether the market lies (partially or in total) in a battleground state. In generating the predicted lines in the figure, we held all of the independent variables at their mean values, varying only Kerry's vote percentage in the 2004 presidential election.

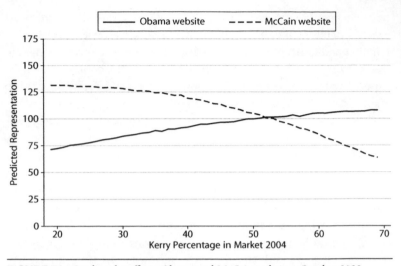

FIGURE 7.1   Predicted traffic to Obama and McCain websites, October 2008

Source: Experian Hitwise.

Note: Results are from multivariate models controlling for media-market demographics.

than the slope of the Obama line, which we might reasonably expect, given that Obama had a wide-ranging online mobilization strategy (Plouffe 2009) that likely reached a far wider audience than McCain's, which was more traditional.

The overall pattern in Figure 7.1 suggests what we expected: that those who visit candidates' websites by and large are not visiting both candidates' websites to seek out information that will help them make a voting choice. Rather, people are more likely to be visiting just one website: that of the candidate they are already inclined to support. As a consequence, scholars must be careful not to overstate the persuasive potential of Internet campaigning. That said, our evidence for this claim is not definitive. We have here only an aggregated measure of visits to the candidates' websites. Moreover, YouTube, political blogs, and online newspapers are excluded.

We also suggest that people who seek out ads online are likely to have much higher political interest on average than those who see ads as a byproduct of watching *Jeopardy* or reruns of *The Family Guy.* For example, Matthew Hindman's *The Myth of Digital Democracy* (2008) finds very little evidence that political blogs and online political media reach beyond partisan (disproportionately liberal) and politically knowledgeable voters. Indeed, the Internet appears to have widened the knowledge gap between those who are interested in politics and those who are not (Prior 2007). Because of their relatively high levels of political sophistication, these online-ad viewers have a greater ability to reject the claims of ads that are inconsistent with their own political predispositions. As we found in Chapter 6, those who are lower in political information are more likely to be persuaded by political advertising.

The limit of online advertising as a persuasion tool is true both for ads placed on the candidates' websites and for their banner advertisements—the ads seen by readers of political and nonpolitical websites that scroll along the top or side or follow the cursor as you wave it over the screen. Political actors are increasingly turning to banner or display ads because they can be targeted to specific websites that reach a target demographic. If, for example, Barack Obama wants to reach out to female voters, he might purchase banner ads on websites read by a disproportionate number of women, such as iVillage.com or Self.com. Furthermore, the ads can be targeted to various zip codes. This is a continuation of the trend noted in Chapter 1 toward micro-targeting, in which campaigns look for specific voters with specific interests and target them with specific appeals. In fact, the term for such online activity is "nano-targeting."

Campaigns have also increased their reliance on "search advertising," where ads appear alongside a viewer's search results, or where relevant web pages appear at the top of the list of results. Traditionally, for example, if a consumer were researching which car to buy and using Google to find the best foreign-made hybrid, Toyota or Volkswagen might peg its ads or website to appear with such a query. Campaigns in 2008 ramped up their use of this tactic.

On the one hand, this is a highly efficient use of resources, as campaigns pay for search and banner ads only if viewers click on the ad. And the possibility exists, of course, for such ads to reach undecided voters. For example, imagine a voter who was unfamiliar with Governor Sarah Palin in the first few days after she was selected as McCain's running mate. A swing voter might search for her on Google and be steered toward an advertisement or website that highlighted her qualifications. This is what campaigns work to do with search-based advertising—increase the odds that a relevant search on a candidate or issue will drive searches to a website or compel them to click on an online ad.

Many online media evangelists see this as the future of campaign advertising. As viewers opt out of watching television in the traditional sense, and skip advertisements more generally by using digital video recorders and TiVo, the advertising industry—and political campaigns—are working hard to reach potential consumers and voters. To be sure, the example of the undecided voter above is a strong case for the potential of online media to persuade voters. But this voter is greatly outnumbered by online users who are strongly attached to political parties and who use the Internet to find the candidates they already support. Campaigns recognize this reality. According to Kaye (2009, 75), "While search ads [in 2008] were used throughout the election season to steer voters toward education information about the candidates, to help them find nearby polling places, to promote local events, or to counteract smears, the main reason for using search was—you guessed it—list building to facilitate fund-raising."

This reality is ever changing, of course, and at some point in the future campaigns will more equally balance persuasion and mobilization goals online, just as they do now in their use of offline resources. But televised political advertising in the traditional sense is as relevant today as a vote-getting tool as it was before political campaigns took to the web, and this is likely to remain true for a number of future election cycles. In general, what holds back the Internet as a vote-getting tool is the fact that people, by and large, must choose to visit campaign websites or seek political ads on YouTube (Morris 1999), whereas television ads come unannounced and without any effort on the part of the viewer.

Parting Remarks

This chapter has shown that exposure to political advertising takes place in many ways. In addition to the traditional means by which viewers watch paid political ads during commercial breaks on television, people are increasingly exposed to coverage of political advertising through news media coverage, and they can access political advertising through the Internet. In spite of increases in ad coverage over time and the availability of new avenues of ad dissemination, we believe that traditional television advertising still has the most impact on shaping citizens' voting choices and candidate evaluations. Our attempt to measure the influence of ad coverage—certainly the most sophisticated to date—revealed that it was paid advertising that was moving votes, not ad coverage. So while we certainly do not discount the possibility that ad coverage or Internet dissemination of advertising may be having some persuasive impact—and that its impact might become greater in the future—the bulk of advertising's impact appears to lie with the traditional paid political ad.

8 ❯ The Future Study of Ad Effects

THE CORE MESSAGE of this book is that televised political advertising influences the choices voters make at the ballot box. This is true despite the recent rise of Internet-based politics. Beyond demonstrating the simple presence of advertising effects, though, our goal was to show that the extent of advertising's influence varies depending on the context of the race, the characteristics of the advertising itself, and the characteristics of the receiver of the message. We have succeeded in finding some ad effects that are contingent, but we have also shown that some ad effects are quite widespread. We will briefly review the findings of the previous chapters.

We discovered in Chapter 4 that, first and foremost, exposure to political advertising does influence the votes that people cast. This was true even in presidential general election races, where ad effects argu ably should be least evident, given relatively balanced message flows and high degrees of knowledge among citizens about the candidates. The strength of advertising's influence does vary across race contexts, however. Ads have greater influence, for example, in highly competitive races. This makes sense if voters are paying more attention during races that feature an intense message environment. Ads also have a greater influence on voting for Senate challengers as opposed to incumbents, which also makes sense, given that less is initially known about challengers.

In Chapter 5, we discovered that both tone-based and emotion-based accounts have limitations in explaining how the characteristics of advertising matter for voting choice. More specifically, our pattern of results was inconsistent across races, with fear and anger ads sometimes working as their sponsors intended and sometime provoking a backlash. Sometimes, exposure to negative or contrast ads worked in favor of their sponsors, and sometimes they were simply ineffective. The good news for candidates and their political allies is that promotional advertising in general, and appeals to enthusiasm specifically, never resulted in a backlash. Despite a pattern of mixed findings, however, we did find that the intended effects model received the bulk of empirical support.

We discovered in Chapter 6 that ad effects were also more widespread than we had predicted. One effect we did expect, however: ads were persuasive even for those who were low in political knowledge. This may be, in part, because of the nature of the message that the typical ad conveys: it is short, simple, and to the point and backed by narration, visuals, and music. Normatively, this is not a bad thing in today's environment, in which political novices are increasingly ignored by campaigns that have shifted their mobilization and targeting efforts to core supporters or regular voters (Goldstein and Ridout 2002)—precisely those citizens who tend to know more about politics. Thus, political ads keep novices connected to elections.

In addition, partisans seem as, or even more, responsive to political advertising than political independents. Although dosage-resistance models, such as Zaller's, suggest that because independents lack partisan anchors, they should be influenced the most by advertising, we found that this was not the case. Indeed, while we found many instances in which advertising reinforced people's partisan predispositions, we also found a number of instances in which Republicans seemed open to Democrats' messages and Democrats seemed open to Republicans' messages. This implies that voters are not automatically rejecting messages from the opposing political camp, perhaps because these ads take pains to avoid identifying the party of the sponsoring candidate and perhaps because campaigns are making specific appeals to voters of the other party on so-called wedge issues (Hillygus and Shields 2009).

Finally, in Chapter 7 we tested the idea that it is not just paid advertising that influences voting choices. News media coverage of advertising has that potential, as well, and this has become more frequent in recent years. We were curious whether the media's continued fascination with discussing candidates' political advertising would translate into persuasion. We were unable to find empirical support for this idea, however, in our omnibus tests of ad coverage's influence. We nonetheless do not discount the possibility that certain "sticky" ads that generate a frenzy of media attention, such as the Swift Boat ads in 2004, have the potential to sway a lot of voters—and at not much cost to the sponsor.

Our total set of findings do not suggest a unifying theory of the influence of political advertising. Sometimes our expectations were clearly affirmed, such as with the strong ad effects in open-seat races and for challengers. But sometimes our predictions were refuted, such as our expectation of minimal ad effects in presidential races and for political partisans. On the latter point, we were simply wrong. We are not dismayed or disillusioned, however. The larger message we draw from this is that political advertising is broadly influential in American politics and for a wide segment of the voting public—certainly a wider segment and a broader array of contexts than we initially expected.

Where we are dismayed, however—and where we were hoping for clarity—is in the mix of findings from Chapter 5. In many ways, our findings mirror the general inferences drawn from the very deep existing scholarship on the effects of negativity in American politics. More specifically, as Lau, Sigelman, and Rovner (2007) have demonstrated, whether negative ads "work" in persuading voters is simply not known. Some studies show a clear intended effect, and some show a backlash. Many have worked to find more consistent patterns, and we hoped to do so by adding a consideration of fear, anger, and enthusiasm ads. Unfortunately, adding emotions to the mix does little to clarify the impact of ads' characteristics, but it also does no worse.

It may be the case that the influence of tone or emotional appeals is so contingent as to be nearly unpredictable. Maybe it is not that certain types of ads work better than certain other types but that certain individual ads work better than others. Or, at the very least, it may be that the content of ads is too difficult to categorize effectively.

Tone may be too broad a concept, and emotion may be too subjective. At the very least, we can use this lack of clarity to suggest future research on the persuasive effects of political advertising.

Future Research on Advertising and Persuasion

In the first chapter of this book, we outlined what we believed were the drawbacks in the study of the persuasive power of political advertising, and we have taken pains to address them. One of our critiques was that insufficient work has examined the impact of political advertising outside of the laboratory in the real world, so we have focused on dozens of real campaigns—U.S. Senate, presidential primary, and presidential general election—in two different election years, with an additional focus in Chapter 7 on a handful of Senate elections in 2006. By making use of panel data, we have been able to make a fairly strong case for causality, the most important strength of experimental research.

Yet many fruitful avenues to study ad persuasion remain. First, as we noted above, although Chapter 5 hints that the study of emotional appeals is a promising possibility, it admittedly does not resolve the question of which advertising appeals work best. Moreover, although we have considered the impact of several of the most common emotional appeals contained in political ads—anger, fear, and enthusiasm—these are obviously not the only appeals that ads contain. One might examine, for instance, whether compassion, pride, or sadness affect an ad's persuasiveness. We caution, however, that coding the presence of such appeals is often challenging.

We have also ignored the potential impact of exposure to ads with varying uses of music and imagery. Are negative messages with ominous music more influential than contrast spots that contain a lot of policy-related evidence and a crescendo of uplifting music? We encourage more investigation in this area.

A third area for additional research could be how an ad's characteristics, the receiver's characteristics, and the campaign context all interact to influence political persuasion. Given the limited sample of respondents and campaign contexts, we were forced to keep our study of these different influences separate. One might hypothesize, however, that anger appeals are most effective when aimed at those who are low in political sophistication in highly competitive races, or that enthusiasm appeals work best with strong partisans in races in which the candidate of one's party is leading. The possibilities here are immense.

To research questions such as these, though, one would need a larger sample of respondents (tens of thousands to really do it right) and a large variety of race contexts (perhaps dozens of U.S. Senate races over several years). Although such large-scale surveys do exist, they often do not contain the instruments needed to create reliable measures of ad exposure—that is, media consumption questions that can account for the likelihood that someone sees an ad.

Following directly from the discussion in Chapter 7, one other area in which there is great potential for the study of ad persuasion is how news coverage of advertising affects voters. We have highlighted the growing coverage of campaign advertisements in the news media, and we have performed the first non-experimental test of ad coverage's impact on voters. Still, this only scratches the surface. Given the dearth of research in this area, the time is right to bring to bear experimental research as well as survey-based evidence to the problem.

All told, the study of advertising persuasion leaves open countless possibilities for additional work, and we hope to continue the work started with this book—and hope others will, as well.

Advertising and Democratic Accountability

We have found that televised political advertising influences people's voting choices, and more specifically, we have shown that ads are having their greatest influence on those who are the least informed about politics. What does this mean for democratic accountability in the United States? We end the book with this important consideration.

On the one hand, if potential voters are learning about the candidates through political advertising—and what they are learning is accurate—then advertising would seem to help voters make "better" choices, choices in line with their own political predispositions. On the other hand, if advertising is "manipulating," making people vote for candidates they otherwise would not—either by presenting false information or by leading people to base their voting choices on "issues" that are irrelevant—then advertising would seem to be more democratic bane than boon.

We fall on the side of the optimists. For one, research—some of it our own—generally suggests that people do learn from political advertising (Brians and Wattenberg 1996; Franz, Freedman, Goldstein, and Ridout 2007; Patterson and McClure 1976; Ridout, Shah, Goldstein, and Franz 2004; Zhao and Chaffee 1995). And although a thirty-second spot does not provide room for a candidate to give a detailed explanation of her twenty-three-point plan to reform the health-care system, a lot of policy-relevant information is nonetheless conveyed in the typical ad. Geer (2006), for instance, reports that about 80 percent of negative appeals and 70 percent of positive appeals in U.S. presidential ads in 2000 contained mentions of issues. It is simply not the case that most ads are mudslinging, talking about the opponent's personality or personal foibles. The sort of information that voters are picking up from ads is the sort of information that allows them to more accurately place a candidate on a liberal–conservative scale (Franz, Freedman, Goldstein, and Ridout 2007), answer correctly questions about facts contained within the ads (Ridout, Shah, Goldstein, and Franz 2004), and increase knowledge of candidates' positions on issues (Brians and Wattenberg 1996).

While the potential always exists for ads to confuse voters or misrepresent the truth, of course, there is not much evidence that they do, despite the anecdote that almost every citizen willingly offers about an ad that seemed beyond the pale. Because television ads are publicly broadcast, the ability of ad sponsors to lie outright is weakened. And any ad from one candidate or party can always be countered with an ad from the opposing candidate or party. This is a particular strength of television compared with other forms of campaigning.

Keep in mind also that factual misrepresentations are possible in all forms of campaign discourse, whether taking place online, on television, or at a town hall meeting. Indeed, it would seem that videos resembling political ads available on the Internet would have much more potential to mislead than ads aired on a broadcast television station. Internet "ads" are unregulated by the Federal Communications Commission, often are not designed or produced by the campaigns themselves, and seldom can be fully erased from the realm of cyber-space. A technologically savvy fourteen-year-old can produce an ad filled with misrepresentations and post it on YouTube in the course of a few hours. That just is not possible for an ad aired on broadcast television.

In short, the often heard claim that television ads—and negativity, more specifically—weakens a healthy debate about issue positions is also not accurate. There are many ads that highlight issue positions, and a negative campaign does not preclude this. We take from this a healthy optimism that campaign advertising, from first principles, represents a body of compelling information that might work to help voters make informed choices.

For those who worry that political advertising—and, in particu-lar, negative political advertising—has too much influence on voters' choices, we offer some reassurance. First, while advertising does have an impact on voting choice, the magnitude of that impact is not huge. We, too, might be worried if exposure to political advertising through-out a campaign made 80 percent of the electorate shift their voting choices, but that is just not the case. Consistent with past research (Shaw 1999, 2006), our findings suggest that the impact of advertising on voting choice is real, but the impact is not massive. Consider spe-cifically the discussion at the end of Chapter 4 in which we estimated the impact of political ads on county-level voting returns in 2000, 2004, and 2008.

But maybe people are being scared into voting for or against par-ticular candidates through attacks or frightening visuals and music? Our results in Chapter 5 do not particularly suggest that negative ads or even contrast ads are any more effective than positive ads in per-suading people to vote for one candidate over another. Even though exposure to negative ads predicted voting choice in some of our models, it did not in others. And exposure to positive ads just as often predicted voting choice. Moreover, our findings from that chap-ter with regard to the impact of certain emotional appeals do not support the claim that anger or fear appeals work better than enthu-siasm appeals in attracting voters, for while exposure to anger appeals explained voting choice in some instances—and exposure to fear appeals persuaded in other instances—the pattern was not consistent across races. Just as often, it was exposure to enthusiasm appeals that moved voting choice.

Ultimately, we believe that campaign ads are important to the democratic process. We would not be troubled, however, if negative advertising were replaced by more serious campaign discussions. In fact, we would rejoice. But campaign ads as they currently exist are not signs of a weakness in American democracy. In fact, as our results confirm, ads rarely shake people from their initial partisan inclinations, and even if they do, ads only accelerate the process, as opposed to initiate it. Ads also help speak to the less informed—a portion of the electorate that is too often ignored by today's campaigns, which are focused on micro-targeting and the activation of core supporters. Ads speak to a wide swath of the electorate and give all voters a chance to encounter campaigns.

We are eager consumers of political advertising, and we enjoy discussing (with each other, with family and friends, and with students) the latest and flashiest political ads. We have devoted years to watching and re-watching the ads, linking them with survey data, and isolating their realized impact on voting citizens. It is true that campaign ads can often annoy us (we roll our eyes often), and many voters end up seeing certain ads dozens of times. But at the end of the day, voters are listening, and the messages break through. Such an influence is a triumph of free elections. We choose to embrace that reality.

APPENDIX A

Variable Coding

2000 Annenberg Panel Surveys

Initial Bush–McCain vote (pre–Super Tuesday): Two binary measures for a respondent's preference of Bush or McCain. Undecided voters and initial supporters of Steve Forbes and Alan Keyes are the base category.

Initial Gore–Bradley vote (pre–Super Tuesday): Two binary measures for a respondent's preference of Gore or Bradley. Undecided voters are the base category.

Bush (Gore) vote (post–Super Tuesday): Reported voting choice. 0 = McCain (Bradley); 1 = Bush (Gore); other = missing

Initial candidate favorability (pre–Super Tuesday): Scaled 0–100

Candidate favorability (post–Super Tuesday): Scaled 0–100

Clinton favorability (pre–Super Tuesday): Scaled 0–100

Education: 1 = grade eight or lower; 2 = some high school, no diploma; 3 = high school diploma or equivalent; 4 = technical or vocational school after high school; 5 = some college, no degree; 6 = associate or two-year college degree; 7 = four-year college degree; 8 = graduate or professional school after college; 9 = graduate or professional degree

Age: In years

Female: Is the respondent female? Coded 0 or 1.

Georgia: Is the respondent from Georgia? Coded 0 or 1.

Married: Is the respondent married? Coded 0 or 1. All responses besides currently married are coded 0.

African American: Does respondent report being African American? Coded 0 or 1.

Party identification: Two binary measures for weak and strong Democrats (and Republicans) and one additional binary measure for independent (strong and not-very-strong identifiers).

Ideology: From liberal to conservative. 1 = very liberal; 2 = liberal; 3 = moderate; 4 = conservative; 5 = very conservative

Local TV news watching: How many days in the past week have you watched the local news? Scaled 0–7

2000 National Election Studies

Nancy Burns, Donald R. Kinder, Steven J. Rosenstone, Virginia Sapiro, and the National Election Studies, "National Election Studies, 2000: Pre-/Post-Election Study," dataset, Center for Political Studies, University of Michigan, Ann Arbor, 2001.

Presidential candidate likes (pre-election): Number of pro-Gore and pro-Bush mentions.

> v000306–v000310: "Is there anything in particular about Vice President Al Gore that might make you want to vote for him? (What is that?)" Up to five mentions

> v000318–v000322: "Is there anything in particular about Texas Governor George W. Bush that might make you want to vote for him? (What is that?)" Up to five mentions

Presidential candidate dislikes (pre-election): Number of anti-Gore and anti-Bush mentions.

> v000312–v000316: "Is there anything in particular about Vice President Al Gore that might make you want to vote against him? (What is that?)" Up to five mentions

> v000324–v000328: "Is there anything in particular about Texas Governor George W. Bush that might make you want to vote against him? (What is that?)" Up to five mentions

Presidential vote intent (pre-election): v000793: "Who do you think you will vote for in the election for president?" Two binary measures for initial Bush or Gore preference. Undecided voters are the base category.

Presidential vote in 2000 (post-election): v001249 (if respondent voted for president): "Who did you vote for?" 0 = Bush; 1 = Gore; other = missing

Senate feeling thermometers (post-election): v001301, Democrat; v001302, Republican

Senate vote in 2000 (post-election): v001275: 0 = Republican; 1 = Democrat; other = missing

Age: v000908: In years

African American: v001006: "What racial or ethnic group or groups best describes you?" 0 = not African American; 1 = African American

Sex: v001029: 0 = male; 1 = female

Income: v000994: Annual household income at category midpoints and with missing values given a value of $53,488 (variable mean)

Education: v000913: 1 = eighth grade or less; 2 = ninth to eleventh grade; 3 = high school diploma or equivalency; 4 = more than twelve years of schooling; 5 = junior college or community college level; 6 = bachelor's degree level; 7 = advanced degree

South: v000080: 0 = respondent lives outside the South; 1 = respondent lives in the South (Alabama, Arkansas, Florida, Georgia, Louisiana, Mississippi, North Carolina, South Carolina, Tennessee, Texas, Virginia)

California: v000080: 0 = respondent lives outside California; 1 = respondent lives in California

Married: v000909: "Are you married now and living with your (husband or wife)—or are you widowed, divorced, separated, or have you never married?" 0 = respondent is not married; 1 = the respondent is married

Party identification: v000523: 0–6 scale, ranging from strong Democrat to strong Republican. We created four binary measures for weak and strong Democrats and Republicans.

Ideology: v000446: 1–7 scale, ranging from very liberal to very conservative

Sociotropic economic evaluations: v000491: "Would you say that over the past year the nation's economy has gotten worse, gotten better, or stayed about the same?" 1 = much better; 2 = somewhat better; 3 = stayed about the same; 4 = somewhat worse; 5 = much worse

Clinton approval: v000341: Pre-election, four-category variable measuring how strongly the respondent approved or disapproved of the job Bill Clinton was doing. "Do you approve or disapprove of the way Bill Clinton is handling his job as president? Strongly or not strongly?"

General political information: How many times (out of six) did the respondent answer the following questions correctly?

v001446–v001457: Now we have a set of questions concerning various public figures. We want to see how much information about them gets out to the public from television, newspapers, and the like.

- ❖ The first name is Trent Lott. What job or political office does he *now* hold?
- ❖ William Rehnquist. What job or political office does he *now* hold?
- ❖ Tony Blair. What job or political office does he *now* hold?
- ❖ Janet Reno. What job or political office does she *now* hold?

v001356–v001357: Do you happen to know which party had the most members in the House of Representatives [U.S. Senate] in Washington *before* the election (this/last) month?

2004 BYU–UW Study

Center for the Study of Elections and Democracy, Brigham Young University, Provo, Utah, and Wisconsin Advertising Project, University of Wisconsin, Madison, "The 2004 Election Panel Study," electronic resources, produced and distributed by Wisconsin Advertising Project, 2004, waves 1–3, available online at http://csp.polisci.wisc.edu/BYU_UW.

Presidential vote intent (wave 1 and wave 2): "If the election for president were held today, who would you vote for?" Two binary measures for initial Bush or Kerry preference. Undecided voters are the base category.

Presidential vote (wave 3): "In the November general election for president, who did you vote for?" 0 = Bush; 1 = Kerry; other = missing

Senate vote intent (wave 1 and wave 2): "If the election for Senate were held today, who would you vote for?" Two binary measures for initial Democratic or Republican preference. Undecided voters are the base category.

Senate vote (wave 3): "In the election for U.S. Senate, who did you vote for?" 0 = Republican candidate; 1 = Democratic candidate; other = missing

Kerry (Bush) favorability (waves 1–3): "Is your opinion of [Bush, Kerry] very favorable . . . very unfavorable?" Ranging from −2 (very unfavorable) to 2 (very favorable)

Democratic (Republican) Senate candidate favorability (waves 1–3): "Is your opinion of [partisan Senate candidate] very favorable . . . very unfavorable?" Ranging from −2 (very unfavorable) to 2 (very favorable)

Bush job approval (wave 3): "How would you rate the overall job President George W. Bush is doing as president: excellent, pretty good, only fair, or poor?" 1–4 scale, with 4 indicating "excellent"

Educational attainment (wave 1): "What is the highest level of education you completed?" 1 = elementary school only; 2 = some high school, did not finish; 3 = completed high school; 4 = some college, didn't finish; 5 = two-year college degree; 6 = four-year college degree; 7 = some graduate work; 8 = completed master's or professional degree; 9 = advanced graduate work or Ph.D.

Age (wave 1): In years

South: 0 = respondent lives outside the South; 1 = respondent lives in the South (Alabama, Arkansas, Florida, Georgia, Louisiana, Mississippi, North Carolina, South Carolina, Tennessee, Texas, Virginia, Kentucky, Maryland, Oklahoma, West Virginia)

Married (wave 1): "Are you currently married, widowed, divorced, separated, or never been married?" 0 = not married; 1 = married

African American (wave 1): "Would you describe yourself as white, black, Asian, Hispanic, American Indian, other?" 0 = not black; 1 = black

Sex (wave 1): 0 = male; 1 = female

Party identification (wave 3): Branching questions were used to create four dummy variables: strong Democrat, weak Democrat, weak Republican, and strong Republican

Ideology (wave 2): "Do you consider yourself generally liberal, moderate, or conservative?" −1 = conservative; 0 = moderate; 1 = liberal

Sociotropic economic evaluation. "Would you say that over the past year the nation's economy has gotten worse, gotten better, or stayed about the same?" 1 = gotten worse; 2 = stayed about the same; 3 = gotten better

General political information (wave 1): How many times (out of four) did the respondent answer the following questions correctly?

- ◆ What job or political office does Bill Frist now hold?
- ◆ What job or political office does William Rehnquist now hold?
- ◆ What job or political office does Tony Blair now hold?
- ◆ What job or political office does John Ashcroft now hold?

2006 Cooperative Congressional Election Study (Wisconsin/UCLA component)

Senate vote: "For whom did you vote in the race for US Senate?" 0 = Republican candidate; 1 = Democratic candidate

Initial Senate preference: "For which candidate do you intend to vote in the race for U.S. Senate?" 0 = Republican candidate; 1 = Democratic candidate.

Education: 1 = no high school; 2 = high school graduate; 3 = some college; 4 = two-year college degree; 5 = four-year college degree; 5 = postgraduate education

Age: In years

Sex: 0 = female; 1 = male

White: 0 = non-white; 1 = white

Annual household income: 1 = less than \$10,000; 2 = \$10,000–\$14,999; 3 = \$15,000–\$19,999; 4 = \$20,000–\$24,999; 5 = \$25,000–\$29,999; 6 = \$30,000–\$39,999; 7 = \$40,000–\$49,999; 8 = \$50,000–\$59,999; 9 = \$60,000–\$69,999; 10 = \$70,000–\$79,999; 11 = \$80,000–\$99,999; 12 = \$100,000–\$119,999; 13 = \$120,000–\$149,999; 14 = \$150,000 or more

Married: 0 = unmarried; 1 = married

Party identification: "In politics, do you think of yourself as a Democrat, a Republican, or an independent?" If Democrat or Republican: "How strongly do you feel about your party?" If independent: "Do you lean toward one of the parties?" 1 = strong Democrat; 2 = weak Democrat; 3 = lean Democrat; 4 = independent; 5 = lean Republican; 6 = weak Republican; 7 = strong Republican

Other Data

General election visits to media markets in 2000, 2004, and 2008: Data for 2000 are reported by Eric M. Appleman of George Washington University at http://www.gwu.edu/~action (accessed June 10, 2004); candidates' travel data for 2004 are reported by the same author at https://www.gwu.edu/~action/2004 (accessed June 7, 2005); and for 2008 at http://www.gwu.edu/~action/P2008 .html (accessed February 12, 2009). Appleman uses public schedules provided by the campaigns supplemented by press accounts to record the city or cities in which the presidential candidates made public appearances on each day. We matched each city with its media market to calculate the total number of visits by each candidate to each media market. We do not count totals visits to a media market in which a candidate attended *only* a fundraiser, because fundraisers generally attract a relatively small number of attendees and are not well reported on by the local news media.

Senate incumbent Democrat in 2000, 2004, and 2008: Federal Election Commission

Senate incumbent Republican in 2000, 2004, and 2008: Federal Election Commission

Senate Republican spending per capita in 2000, 2004, and 2008: Federal Election Commission

Senate Democrat spending per capita in 2000, 2004, and 2008: Federal Election Commission

County-level presidential and Senate vote returns: Dave Leip's Atlas of Presidential Elections, available online at http://uselectionatlas.org

County-level demographics: Annual Current Population Survey, available online at http://www.census.gov/popest/counties

County-level median income: U.S. Census Bureau, "Small Area Income and Poverty Estimates," available online at http://www.census.gov/did/www/saipe/index.html

APPENDIX B

Full Model Results from Chapter 4

Note: In all of the tables in this appendix, with the exception of the county-level models, we report only the z-scores for all control variables. This is meant to minimize the clutter in the tables. It also conveys the basic information that is most important to the reader: statistical significance. Coefficient estimates for all of the control variables are available on request from the authors.

TABLE B.1 Full Model Results from Table 4.1, Presidential General Election

	2004			2000				
	Vote Kerry	Kerry favorability	Bush favorability	Vote Gore	Gore likes	Gore dislikes	Bush likes	Bush dislikes
Initial Kerry (Gore) vote	1.99			5.65				
Initial Bush vote	-2.2			-5.19				
Initial favorability		8.24	7.29					
Kerry (Gore) ad exposure	1.96	2.63	-1.02	0.03	2.62	1.59	0.35	2.92
Bush exposure	-2.96	-2.65	1.21	0.44	-1.68	-0.5	0.63	-1.54
Age	-2.48	-1.24	0.88	-0.35	1.76	1.41	1.32	2.49
Age-squared	2.3	1.64	-0.74	0.35	-1.42	1.35	-0.81	-2.51
Education	1.34	0.72	1.02	1.28	5.38	5.22	3.23	7.06
South	-0.55	0.55	2.45	0.14	-0.06	0.3	3.5	-2.1
Married	-1.13	-0.12	0.5	-0.04	-0.76	-1.11	0.81	-1.02
African American	1.16	0.65	-0.98	2.45	-1.26	-1.03	-0.56	-0.67
Female	-2.31	-1.37	0.71	0.93	0.95	-1.47	0.36	-2.45
Weak Democrat	1.14	0.25	-0.76	1.15	2.75	-2.19	-1.93	1.13
Weak Republican	-3.7	-0.37	1.34	-2.4	-2.12	0.08	2.94	-3.38
Strong Democrat	2.4	3.63	-1.25	1.55	6.73	-5.24	-4.31	3.97
Strong Republican	-2.44	-0.38	3.6	-4.19	-2.99	3.9	5.04	-3.13
Conservative (2000); liberal (2004)	1.79	2.02	-0.89	-2.23	-1.64	1.6	5.25	-3.09
Economic assessment	-0.27	-0.55	0.36	-0.43	-2.67	1.76	-0.9	-1.04

Bush visits	1.94	1.48	-1.25	-0.93	0.67	-0.53	-2.53	1
Kerry (Gore) visits	-0.79	0.73	1.7	1.16	0.52	-1.12	-1.34	0.83
Bush (Clinton) job approval	-5.94	-2.9	8.89	3.3	7.95	-6.71	-6.66	4.6
California				2	1.58	-0.73	-0.45	1.65
Constant	4.64			-0.14	-7	-4.38	-5.11	-6.16
N	922	986	1,000	783	1,055	1,055	1,055	1,055
Model estimation	logit	ordered probit	ordered probit	logit	GLM	GLM	GLM	GLM

Survey: 2000 ANES and 2004 BYU–UW panel study. Entries are z-scores. There is no constant for favorability models because the ordered probit model estimates thresholds, which are not shown here. A California binary measure is included in the 2000 models to account for an unexpected ad buy by George Bush in the final weeks of the election.

TABLE B.2 Full Model Results for Table 4.2, 2000 Presidential Primary

	Vote Bush	Vote Gore	Bush favorability	McCain favorability	Gore favorability	Bradley favorability
Initial Bush (Gore) vote	5.27	8.33				
Initial McCain (Bradley) vote	-6.43	-4.15				
Initial favorability			10.24	14.72	12.25	14.15
Bush (Gore) ad exposure	-0.06	3.02	1.04	0.81	0.76	1.6
McCain (Bradley) ad exposure	0.18	-2.17	-0.77	-0.88	-1.17	-0.11
Clinton favorability	-0.46	1.23	-6.3	-0.26	7.74	-1.89
Education	-2.51	-0.9	-2.96	0.33	0.25	3.38
Age	-0.22	-1.94	-0.69	0.95	-2.57	-1.67
Age-squared	-0.03	2.05	0.38	-0.61	2.43	1.87
Female	0.49	-1.82	-3.01	-0.61	0.28	0.29
Georgia	5.85		-1.49	-2.98	-4.54	-1.56
Married	1.43	-1.98	1.32	-0.1	0.92	1.66
African American	1.13	2.21	1.45	0.36	1.83	-0.67
Independent	2.13	0.89	0.49	0.97	2.07	-2.37
Weak Republican (Democrat)	2.56	0.56	2.21	0.15	3.99	-2.04
Strong Republican (Democrat)	3.24	1.04	2.6	-0.01	4.21	-0.69
Ideology (liberal to conservative)	4.08	-0.06	4.18	-1.34	-0.65	-2.37
Local TV news watching	0.6	2	0.2	1.89	2.03	-1.1
Constant	-0.77	1.72	5.26	2.7	6.28	7.34
N	571	513	918	808	931	797
Model estimation	logit	logit	OLS	OLS	OLS	OLS

Survey: National Annenberg Super Tuesday Panel Study. Entries are z-scores. Georgia is included as a dummy variable because it is the only southern state on Super Tuesday. It drops from the Vote Gore model because there is no variation.

TABLE B.3 Full Model Results from Table 4.3, Senate General Election

	2004			2000		
	Vote Democrat	Democratic favorability	Republican favorability	Vote Democrat	Democratic feeling thermometer	Republican feeling thermometer
Initial Democratic vote	2.16					
Initial Republican vote	-2.07					
Initial favorability		10.66	6.94			
Democratic ad exposure	1.86	0.34	-1.51	0.72	1.02	0.16
Republican ad exposure	-1.8	-0.84	4.29	-1.69	-1.72	1.1
Age	-0.86	-0.43	0.64	0.45	-0.16	-1.51
Age-squared	0.67	0.59	-0.56	-0.54	0.99	1.67
Education	-1.59	-0.13	1.12	-0.35	-0.91	-2.44
Income				-0.16	0.63	1.65
South	-0.81	-2.34	-0.24	0.02	2.83	2.61
Married	-0.28	0	-1.15	2.08	0	0.43
African American	0.37	-0.1	0.26	3.21	0.84	-1.21
Female	-0.59	0.27	-0.25	1.53	5.34	-0.09
Weak Democrat	0.95	-0.07	0.11	2.89	2.57	-1.41
Weak Republican	-1.83	-1.25	-0.17	-2.56	0.3	0.74
Strong Democrat	1.91	2.43	-1.9	7.44	8.78	-2.47
Strong Republican	-1.51	-1.42	-0.66	-2.94	-4.08	2.31

(continued on next page)

TABLE B.3 *Continued*

	2004			2000		
	Vote Democrat	Democratic favorability	Republican favorability	Vote Democrat	Democratic feeling thermometer	Republican feeling thermometer
Conservative (2000); liberal (2004)	1.81	0.46	−0.96	−3.67	−2.02	5.08
Economic assessment	−2.08	−0.27	−0.76	−0.19	−1.99	0.7
Incumbent Democrat	−0.28	−1.3	2.59	6.05	2.04	−0.39
Incumbent Republican	−0.07	−3.46	0.68	−2.06	0.76	2.38
Bush (Clinton) job approval	−3.11	−3.97	2.72	7.05	2.54	−2.9
Logged Republican spending per capita				0.36	−0.17	−0.21
Logged Democratic spending per capita				0.222	2.8	−0.86
Total spending per capita				0.27	−2.56	1.62
Constant	2.91			−1.39	4.05	8.36
N	577	415	449	570	665	679
Model estimation	logit	ordered probit	ordered probit	logit	OLS	OLS

Survey: 2000 ANES and 2004 BYU–UW panel study. Entries are z-scores. There is no constant for favorability models because the ordered probit models estimate thresholds, which are not shown here.

TABLE B.4 Full Model Results from Table 4.6, County-Level Vote Simulations

	2000		2004		2008	
	Coefficient	z-score	Coefficient	z-score	Coefficient	z-score
President						
Democratic advertising advantage (October ads)	0.002	8.58	0.001	3.28	0.001	6.04
Democratic visits to market	−0.014	−0.33	−0.036	−0.59	0.248	4.25
Republican visits to market	0.067	1.45	0.113	1.54	−0.201	−4.8
Democratic vote in previous election	0.842	23.31	−0.619	−12.82	−0.421	−3.25
Republican vote in previous election	−0.125	−3.69	−1.540	−33.88	−1.351	−10.54
Percent African American	0.001	0.07	0.040	2.77	0.134	13.12
Percent White	−0.097	−6.72	−0.069	−4.93	−0.024	−2.44
Percent Hispanic	0.045	4.89	0.041	4.92	0.158	23.55
Percent Asian	0.147	3.79	0.219	6.58	−0.003	−0.07
Percent 65 and over	−0.112	−3.35	0.084	2.84	0.139	5.46
Percent 25 and younger	−0.097	−3.73	−0.024	−1	0.223	10.37
Percent male	−0.340	−7.91	−0.081	−2.07	−0.081	−2.8
Median household income ($10,000s)	0.703	6.19	0.211	2.37	1.120	14.06
Constant	36.443	8	158.617	29.44	128.396	9.94

(continued on next page)

TABLE B.4 *Continued*

	2000		2004		2008	
	Coefficient	z-score	Coefficient	z-score	Coefficient	z-score
Senate						
Democratic advertising advantage (October ads)	0.008	3.27	0.005	3.47	0.003	1.89
Democratic incumbent	4.007	1.58	2.933	1.07	7.359	1.48
Republican incumbent	−11.252	−5.73	−3.024	−0.85	−10.809	−3.36
Democratic spending per capita	−1.123	−1.35	4.390	1.87	1.763	2.99
Republican spending per capita	0.176	0.12	−6.340	−3.33	−0.258	−0.18
Democratic presidential vote in previous election	1.208	4.7	0.764	2.17	1.887	1.87
Republican presidential vote in previous election	0.233	0.91	−0.149	−0.44	1.063	1.06
Percent African American	0.184	1.06	0.010	0.13	0.028	0.25
Percent White	0.308	1.59	0.131	1.69	−0.005	−0.07
Percent Hispanic	−0.161	−2.68	−0.143	−2.11	0.132	1.56
Percent Asian	0.184	0.79	0.079	0.57	0.126	0.55
Percent 65 and older	−0.346	−1.34	−0.926	−3.4	0.285	1.48
Percent 25 and younger	0.009	0.06	−0.415	−2.14	0.123	1.03
Percent male	−0.327	−1.31	−0.230	−1.2	−0.048	−0.52
Median household income ($10,000s)	−1.687	−1.93	−1.779	−2.51	−0.792	−1.4
Southern state	−6.099	−2.57	1.107	0.46	5.304	1.28
Constant	−14.329	−0.45	57.397	1.69	−94.801	−0.97

Note: The dependent variable is percentage of Democratic vote in the county. All percentage variables are coded 0–100. The presidential models are estimated with fixed effects for states.

APPENDIX C

Additional Model Results from Chapter 5

TABLE C.1 Favorability Results for Tone

	Democratic exposure			Republican exposure		
	Negative	Contrast	Positive	Negative	Contrast	Positive
2000 Senate						
Dem feeling thermometer	0.05	1.18	0.82	0.33	−0.52	−0.58
Rep feeling thermometer	−0.75	−0.1	0.33	−0.74	−1.54	**3.24**
2004 Senate						
Dem favorability	−1.15	0.29	0.1	0.15	0.15	**−2.82**
Rep favorability	−0.67	−1.09	**−1.77**	0.17	**2.99**	−0.63
2000 presidential						
Gore likes	**1.69**	−1.38	−0.22	0.86	0.47	−1.47
Gore dislikes	1.21	−0.69	0.05	−0.4	1	−0.66
Bush likes	−0.91	−0.3	1.03	1.51	**1.68**	−1.59
Bush dislikes	**3.08**	−0.25	−0.46	−1.42	−0.8	−0.2
2004 presidential						
Kerry favorability	1.36	**2.25**	0.43	−0.72	−0.16	**−2.62**
Bush favorability	−1.28	−1.24	0.95	−0.1	0.54	**1.96**

Survey: 2000 ANES and 2004 BYU–UW panel study. Entries are *z*-scores. Boldface indicates that the variable is statistically significant at the .10 level. The boxed entries represent the results of one model estimation. Each similarly paired entry within tone is from one model run. The models also contain Democrats' and Republicans' exposure to all ads not of that tone. Those exposure results and all other control variables are not shown here. They are available from the authors on request.

TABLE C.2   Favorability Results for Emotions

	Democratic exposure			Republican exposure		
	Fear	Anger	Enthusiasm	Fear	Anger	Enthusiasm
2004 Senate						
Dem favorability	$\boxed{-3.54}$	−1.41	1.22	$\boxed{0.19}$	0.39	0.01
Rep favorability	−0.31	**−1.82**	−0.86	0.15	**2.36**	**2.84**
2004 presidential						
Kerry favorability	**2.5**	**2.93**	**2**	0.54	−0.09	−1.29
Bush favorability	−0.64	−0.35	0.36	−0.44	−0.63	**2.21**

Survey: 2004 BYU–UW panel study. Entries are z-scores. Boldface indicates that the variable is statistically significant at the .10 level. The boxed entries represent the results of one model estimation. Each similarly paired entry within emotion is from one model run. The models also contain Democrats' and Republicans' exposure to all ads not of that emotional appeal. Those exposure results and all other control variables are not shown here. They are available from the authors on request.

References

Addonizio, Elizabeth, Donald Green, and James Glaser. 2007. "Putting the Party Back into Politics: An Experiment Testing whether Election Day Festivals Increase Voter Turnout." *PS: Political Science and Politics* 40(4): 721–727.

Ansolabehere, Stephen, and Shanto Iyengar. 1995. *Going Negative: How Political Advertising Shrinks and Polarizes the Electorate.* New York: Free Press.

———. 1996. "Can the Press Monitor Campaign Advertising? An Experimental Study." *Harvard International Journal of Press/Politics* 1(1): 72–86.

Bartels, Larry. 1988. *Presidential Primaries and the Dynamics of Public Choice.* Princeton, N.J.: Princeton University Press.

———. 2000. "Campaign Quality: Standards for Evaluation, Benchmarks for Reform." In *Campaign Reform: Insights and Evidence,* ed. Larry Bartels and Lynn Vavreck, 1–59. Ann Arbor: University of Michigan Press.

Basil, Michael, Caroline Schooler, and Byron Reeves. 1991. "Positive and Negative Political Advertising: Effectiveness of Ads and Perceptions of Candidates." In *Television and Political Advertising: Psychological Processes,* vol. 1, ed. Frank Biocca, 245–262. Hillsdale, N.J.: Lawrence Erlbaum.

Brader, Ted. 2006. *Campaigning for Hearts and Minds: How Emotional Appeals in Political Ads Work.* Chicago: University of Chicago Press.

Brians, Craig Leonard, and Martin P. Wattenberg. 1996. "Campaign Issue Knowledge and Salience: Comparing Reception from TV Commercials, TV News, and Newspapers." *American Journal of Political Science* 40(1): 172–193.

Brooks, Deborah Jordan, and John G. Geer. 2007. "Beyond Negativity: The Effects of Incivility on the Electorate." *American Journal of Political Science* 51(1): 1–16.

Brunell, Thomas L. 2008. *Redistricting and Representation: Why Competitive Elections Are Bad for America.* New York: Routledge.

Carr, David. 2009. "As TV Dwindles, It Still Leads." *New York Times,* May 24, B1.

Carter, Bill. 2009. "DVR, Once TV's Mortal Foe, Helps Ratings." *New York Times,* November 1, B1.

Chang, Chingching. 2001. "The Impact of Emotion Elicited by Print Political Advertising on Candidate Evaluation." *Media Psychology* 3(2): 91–118.

———. 2003. "Party Bias in Political-Advertising Processing: Results from an Experiment Involving the 1998 Taipei Mayoral Election." *Journal of Advertising* 32(2): 55–67.

Clinton, Joshua, and Andrew Owen. 2006. "An Experimental Investigation of Advertising Persuasiveness: Is Impact in the Eye of the Beholder?" Paper presented at the annual meeting of the Canadian Political Science Association, June 1–3, Toronto.

Downs, Anthony. 1957. *An Economic Theory of Democracy.* New York: Harper.

Djupe, Paul A., and David A. M. Peterson. 2002. "The Impact of Negative Campaigning: Evidence from the 1998 Senatorial Primaries." *Political Research Quarterly* 55(4): 845–860.

Druckman, James N. 2004. "Priming the Vote: Campaign Effects in a U.S. Senate Election." *Political Psychology* 24(4): 577–594.

Fowler, Erika Franklin, and Travis Ridout. 2009. "Local Television and Newspaper Coverage of Political Advertising." *Political Communication* 26(2): 119–136.

Franz, Michael M. 2008. *Choices and Changes: Interest Groups in the Electoral Process.* Philadelphia: Temple University Press.

Franz, Michael, Paul Freedman, Kenneth M. Goldstein, and Travis N. Ridout. 2007. *Campaign Advertising and American Democracy.* Philadelphia: Temple University Press.

———. 2008. "Understanding the Effect of Political Ads on Voter Turnout: A Response to Krasno and Green." *Journal of Politics.* 70(1): 262–268.

Franz, Michael, Joel Rivlin, and Kenneth Goldstein. 2006. "Much More of the Same: Television Advertising Pre- and Post-BCRA." In *The Election after Reform: Money, Politics, and the Bipartisan Campaign Reform Act,* ed. Michael J. Malbin, 139–162. Lanham, Md.: Rowman and Littlefield.

Freedman, Paul, and Ken Goldstein. 1999. "Measuring Media Exposure and the Effects of Negative Campaign Ads." *American Journal of Political Science* 43(4): 1189–1208.

Freedman, Paul, Michael Franz, and Kenneth Goldstein. 2004. "Campaign Advertising and Democratic Citizenship." *American Journal of Political Science* 48(4): 723–741.

Fridkin, Kim L., and Patrick J. Kenney. 2004. "Do Negative Messages Work? The Impact of Negativity on Citizens' Evaluations of Candidates." *American Politics Research* 32(5): 570–605.

————. 2008. "The Dimensions of Negative Messages." *American Politics Research.* 36(5): 694–723.

Garramone, Gina M. 1984. "Voter Responses to Negative Political Ads." *Journalism Quarterly* 61(2): 250–259.

————. 1985. "Effects of Negative Political Advertising: The Roles of Sponsor and Rebuttal." *Journal of Broadcasting and Electronic Media* 29(2): 147–159.

Geer, John G. 2006. *In Defense of Negativity: Attack Ads in Presidential Campaigns.* Chicago: University of Chicago Press.

Geer, John G., and James Geer. 2003. "Remembering Attack Ads: An Experimental Investigation of Radio." *Political Behavior* 25(1): 69–95.

Gertner, Jon. 2004. "The Very, Very Personal Is the Political." *New York Times Sunday Magazine,* February 15, 43.

Goldstein, Ken, and Paul Freedman. 1999. "Measuring Media Exposure and the Effects of Negative Campaign Ads." *American Journal of Political Science* 43(4): 1189–1208.

————. 2000. "New Evidence for New Arguments: Money and Advertising in the 1996 Senate Elections. *Journal of Politics* 62(4): 1087–1108.

————. 2002. "Lessons Learned: Campaign Advertising in the 2000 Elections." *Political Communication* 19:5–28.

Goldstein, Kenneth M., and Travis N. Ridout. 2002. "The Politics of Participation: Mobilization and Turnout over Time." *Political Behavior* 24 (1): 3–29.

Green, Donald P., and Jonathan S. Krasno. 1988. "Salvation for the Spendthrift Incumbent: Reestimating the Effects of Campaign Spending in House Elections." *American Journal of Political Science* 32:884–907.

————. 1990. "Rebuttal to Jacobson's 'New Evidence for Old Arguments.'" *American Journal of Political Science* 34:363–372.

Greenfield, Jeff, and Jerry Bruno. 1972. *The Advance Man.* New York: Bantam.

Groenendyk, Eric W., and Nicholas A. Valentino. 2002. "Of Dark Clouds and Silver Linings: Effects of Exposure to Issue versus Candidate Advertising on Persuasion, Information Retention, and Issue Salience." *Communication Research* 29(3): 295–319.

Haddock, Geoffrey, and Mark P. Zanna. 1993. "Impact of Negative Advertising on Evaluations of Political Candidates: The 1993 Canadian Federal Election." *Basic and Applied Social Psychology* 19(2): 205–223.

Hillygus, D. Sunshine, and Simon Jackman. 2003. "Voter Decision Making in Election 2000: Campaign Effects, Partisan Activation, and the Clinton Legacy." *American Journal of Political Science* 47(4): 583–596.

Hillygus, D. Sunshine, and Todd G. Shields. 2009. *The Persuadable Voter: Wedge Issues in Presidential Campaigns.* Princeton, N.J.: Princeton University Press.

Hindman, Matthew. 2005. "The Real Lessons of Howard Dean: Reflections on the First Digital Campaign." *Perspectives on Politics* 3(1): 121–128.

———. 2008. *The Myth of a Digital Democracy.* Princeton, N.J.: Princeton University Press.

Holbrook, Thomas. 1996. *Do Campaigns Matter?* London: Sage.

Huber, Gregory, and Kevin Arceneaux. 2007. "Identifying the Persuasive Effects of Presidential Advertising." *American Journal of Political Science* 51(4): 957–977.

Huddy, Leonie, Stanley Feldman, and Erin Cassese. 2007. "On the Distinct Political Effects of Anxiety and Anger." In *The Affect Effect: Dynamics of Emotion in Political Thinking and Behavior,* ed. W. Russell Neuman, George E. Marcus, Ann Crigler, and Michael MacKuen, 202–230. Chicago: University of Chicago Press.

Iyengar, Shanto, and Adam F. Simon. 2000. "New Perspectives and Evidence on Political Communication and Campaign Effects." *Annual Review of Psychology* 51(1): 149–169.

Jackson, Robert A., Jeffrey J. Mondak, and Robert Huckfeldt. 2009. "Examining the Possible Corrosive Impact of Negative Advertising on Citizens' Attitudes toward Politics." *Political Research Quarterly* 62(1): 55–69.

Jacobson, Gary C. 2008. *The Politics of Congressional Elections,* 4th ed. New York: Longman.

———. 1990. "The Effects of Campaign Spending in House Elections: New Evidence for Old Arguments." *American Journal of Political Science* 34(2): 334–362.

Jamieson, Kathleen Hall, Paul Waldman, and Susan Sherr. 2000. "Eliminate the Negative? Categories of Analysis for Political Advertisements." In *Crowded Airwaves: Campaign Advertising in Elections,* ed. James A. Thurber, Candice J. Nelson, and David A. Dulio, 44–64. Washington, D.C.: Brookings Institution Press.

Johnston, Richard, Michael G. Hagen, and Kathleen Hall Jamieson. 2004. *The 2000 Presidential Election and the Foundations of Party Politics.* Cambridge: Cambridge University Press.

Kahn, Kim Fridkin, and John G. Geer. 1994. "Creating Impressions: An Experimental Investigation of Political Advertising on Television." *Political Behavior* 16(1): 93–116.

Kahn, Kim Fridkin, and Patrick J. Kenney. 1999. "Do Negative Campaigns Mobilize or Suppress Turnout?" *American Political Science Review* 93(4): 877–890.

———. 2004. *No Holds Barred: Negativity in U.S. Senate Campaigns*. Upper Saddle River, N.J.: Pearson.

Kaid, Lynda Lee. 1997. "Effects of the Television Spots on Images of Dole and Clinton." *American Behavioral Scientist* 40 (August): 1085–1094.

Kaye, Kate. 2009. *Campaign '08: A Turning Point for Digital Media*. Los Angeles: CreateSpace.

Kimball, David C. 2009. "Interest Groups in the 2008 Presidential Election: The Barking Dog That Didn't Bite." *Forum* 6(4): article 2.

Krasno, Jon, and Donald Green. 2008. "Do Televised Presidential Ads Increase Voter Turnout? Evidence from a Natural Experiment." *Journal of Politics* 70(1): 245–261.

Krosnick, Jon A., and Laura A. Brannon. 1993. "The Impact of the Gulf War on the Ingredients of Presidential Evaluations: Multidimensional Effects of Political Involvement." *American Political Science Review* 87(4): 963–975.

Kurtz, Howard. 2008. "Talked-about Ads Were Seldom Aired." *Washington Post*, September 24, A4.

Lau, Richard R., and Gerald M. Pomper. 2004. *Negative Campaigning: An Analysis of U.S. Senate Elections*. Lanham, Md.: Rowman and Littlefield.

Lau, Richard, Lee Sigelman, and Ivy Brown Rovner. 2007. "The Effects of Negative Political Advertisements: A Meta-Analytic Reassessment." *Journal of Politics* 69(4): 1176–1209.

Lawton, L. Dale, and Paul Freedman. 2001. "Beyond Negativity: Advertising Effects in the 2000 Virginia Senate Race." Paper presented at the annual meeting of the Midwest Political Science Association, Chicago, April 19–22.

Lazarsfeld, Paul F., Bernard Berelson, and Hazel Gaudet. 1944. *The People's Choice: How the Voter Makes Up His Mind in a Presidential Campaign*. New York: Duell, Sloan and Pearce.

Leighley, Jan E. 2004. *Mass Media and Politics: A Social Science Perspective*. New York: Houghton Mifflin.

Lemert, James B., Wayne Wanta, and Tien-Tsung Lee. 1999. "Party Identification and Negative Advertising in a U.S. Senate Election." *Journal of Communication* 49(2): 123–134.

Magleby, David. 2004. "The Impact of Issue Advocacy and Party Soft Money Electioneering." In *The Medium and the Message*, ed. Kenneth Goldstein and Patricia Strach, 84–104. Upper Saddle River, N.J.: Pearson.

Marcus, George, and Michael B. MacKuen. 1993. "Anxiety, Enthusiasm, and the Vote: The Emotional Underpinnings of Learning and Involvement during Presidential Campaigns." *American Political Science Review* 87(3): 672–685.

Marcus, George E., W. Russell Neuman, and Michael MacKuen. 2000. *Affective Intelligence and Political Judgment.* Chicago: University of Chicago Press.

Martin, Paul S. 2004. "Inside the Black Box of Negative Campaign Effects: Three Reasons Why Negative Campaigns Mobilize." *Political Psychology* 25(4): 545–562.

McGinnis, Joe. 1969. *The Selling of the President 1968.* New York: Simon and Schuster.

Mendelberg, Tali. 2001. *The Race Card.* Princeton, N.J.: Princeton University Press.

Meirick, Patrick. 2002. "Cognitive Responses to Negative and Comparative Political Advertising." *Journal of Advertising* 31(1): 49–62.

Merritt, Sharyne. 1984. "Negative Political Advertising: Some Empirical Findings." *Journal of Advertising* 13(1): 27–38.

Miller, Joanne M., and Jon A. Krosnick. 2000. "News Media Impact on the Ingredients of Presidential Evaluations: Politically Knowledgeable Citizens Are Guided by a Trusted Source." *American Journal of Political Science* 44(2): 305–315.

Moore, David. 2009. *The Opinion Makers: An Insider Exposes the Truth Behind the Polls.* Boston: Beacon.

Morris, Dick. 1999. *Vote.com.* Los Angeles: Renaissance Books.

Patterson, Thomas E., and Robert D. McClure. 1976. *The Unseeing Eye: The Myth of Television Power in National Elections.* New York: Putnam.

Peterson, David A. M., and Paul A. Djupe. 2005. "When Primary Campaigns Go Negative: The Determinants of Campaign Negativity." *Political Research Quarterly* 58(1): 45–54.

Pfau, Michael, and Michael Louden. 1994. "Effectiveness of Adwatch Formats in Deflecting Political Attack Ads." *Communication Research* 21(3): 325–341.

Pfau, Michael, R. Lance Holbert, Erin A. Szabo, and Kelly Kaminski. 2002. "Issue-Advocacy versus Candidate Advertising: Effects on Candidate Preferences and Democratic Process." *Journal of Communication* 52(2): 301–315.

Pfau, Michael, David Park, R. Lance Holbert, and Jaeho Cho. 2001. "The Effects of Party- and PAC-Sponsored Issue Advertising and the Potential of Inoculation to Combat Its Impact on the Democratic Process." *American Behavioral Scientist* 44(12): 2379–2397.

Pinkleton, Bruce E. 1997. "The Effects of Negative Comparative Political Advertising on Candidate Evaluations and Advertising Evaluations: An Exploration." *Journal of Advertising* 26(1): 19–29.

———. 1998. "Effects of Print Comparative Political Advertising on Political Decision-making and Participation." *Journal of Communication* 48(4): 24–36.

Plouffe, David. 2009. *The Audacity to Win: The Inside Story and Lessons of Barack Obama's Historic Victory.* New York: Viking.

Price, Vincent, and John Zaller. 1993. "Who Gets the News? Alternative Measures of News Reception and Their Implications for Research." *Public Opinion Quarterly* 57(2):133–164.

Prior, Marcus. 2007. *Post-Broadcast Democracy: How Media Choice Increases Inequality in Political Involvement and Polarizes Elections.* Cambridge: Cambridge University Press.

———. 2009. "The Immensely Inflated News Audience: Assessing Bias in Self-Reported News Exposure." *Public Opinion Quarterly* 73(1): 130–143.

"Reds and Blues: States in the Spotlight." 2009. *Politics* (March): 43.

Ridout, Travis N. 2004. "Campaign Advertising Strategies in the 2000 Presidential Nominations: The Case of Al, George, Bill, and John." In *The Medium and the Message,* ed. Kenneth Goldstein and Patricia Strach, 5–26. Upper Saddle River, N.J.: Pearson.

Ridout, Travis N., and Michael M. Franz. 2007. "Do Political Ads Persuade?" *Political Behavior* 29(4): 465–491.

———. 2008. "Evaluating Measures of Campaign Tone." *Political Communication* 25(2): 158–179.

Ridout, Travis N., Dhavan V. Shah, Kenneth M. Goldstein, and Michael M. Franz. 2004. "Evaluating Measures of Campaign Advertising Exposure on Political Learning." *Political Behavior* 26(3): 201–225.

Ridout, Travis N., and Glen R. Smith. 2008. "Free Advertising: How the Media Amplify Campaign Messages." *Political Research Quarterly* 61(4): 598–608.

Rivers, Douglas. 2006. "Sample Matching: Representative Sampling from Internet Panels." White Paper Series, Polimetrix Inc., Palo Alto, Calif.

Rivlin, Joel. 2008. "On the Air: Advertising in 2004 as a Window on the 2008 Presidential Election," *Forum* 5(4): article 7.

Robinson, Michael, and Margaret Sheehan. 1983. *Over the Wire and on TV: CBS and UPI in Campaign '80.* New York: Russell Sage Foundation.

Rutenberg, Jim, and Kate Zernike. 2004. "Going Negative: When It Works." *New York Times,* August 22, sec. 4, 1.

Scott, Douglas R., and Debbie Solomon. 1998. "What Is Wearout Anyway?" *Journal of Advertising Research* 27(5): 19–28.

Shapiro, Michael A., and Robert H. Rieger. 1992. "Comparing Positive and Negative Advertising on Radio." *Journalism Quarterly* 69:135–145.

Shaw, Daron R. 1999. "The Effect of TV Ads and Candidate Appearances on Statewide Presidential Votes, 1988–96." *American Political Science Review* 93(2): 345–361.

———. 2006. *The Race to 270: The Electoral College and the Campaign Strategies of 2000 and 2004.* Chicago: University of Chicago Press.

Sigelman, Lee, and David K. Park. 2007. "Incivility in Presidential Campaigns, 1952–2000." Working paper, George Washington University, Washington, D.C.

Simon, Roger. 2003. "The Doctor Is In—In Your Face! Howard Dean Isn't Afraid of the President, so Why Are Democrats Afraid of Dean?" *U.S. News and World Report,* vol. 135, August 11, 12.

Sniderman, Paul M., Richard A. Brody, and Philip E. Tetlock. 1991. *Reasoning and Choice: Explorations in Political Psychology.* Cambridge: Cambridge University Press.

Sosnik, Doug, Matthew Dowd, and Ron Fournier. 2006. *Applebee's America.* New York: Simon and Schuster.

Steinberg, Jacques, and Bill Carter. 2005. "CBS Dismisses Four over Broadcast on Bush Service." *New York Times,* November 1, A1.

Stelter, Brian. 2009. "Eight Hours a Day Spent on Screens, Study Finds." *New York Times,* March 27, B6.

Stevens, Daniel. 2008. "Measuring Exposure to Political Advertising in Surveys." *Political Behavior* 30(1): 47–72.

———. 2009. "Elements of Negativity: Volume and Proportion in Exposure to Negative Advertising." *Political Behavior* 31(3): 429–451.

Valentino, Nicholas A., Vincent L. Hutchings, and Dimitri Williams. 2004. "The Impact of Political Advertising on Knowledge, Internet Information Seeking, and Candidate Preference." *Journal of Communication* 54(2): 337–354.

Vavreck, Lynn, and Douglas Rivers. 2008. "The 2006 Cooperative Congressional Election Study." *Journal of Elections, Public Opinion, and Policy* 18(4): 355–366.

Wattenberg, Martin. 2010. "The Presidential Media Environment in the Age of Obama." In *Obama: Year One,* ed. Thomas R. Dye, George C. Edwards III, Morris P. Fiorina, Edward S. Greenberg, Paul C. Light, David B. Magleby, and Martin P. Wattenberg. New York: Longman.

West, Darrell M. 2008. *Air Wars: Television Advertising in Election Campaigns, 1952–2000,* 3rd ed. Washington, D.C.: Congressional Quarterly Press.

Wicker, Tom. 1988. "Medium and Message." *New York Times,* November 15, A31.

Winograd, Morley, and Michael Hais. 2008. *Millennial Makeover: MySpace, YouTube, and the Future of American Politics.* New Brunswick, N.J.: Rutgers University Press.

Yeager, David, Jon A. Krosnick, LinChiat Chang, Harold S. Javitz, Matthew S. Levindusky, Alberto Simpser, and Rui Wang. 2009. "Comparing the Accuracy of RDD Telephone Surveys and Internet Surveys Conducted with Probability and Non-Probability Samples." Working paper, Stanford University, Palo Alto, Calif.

Zaller, John. 1992. *The Nature and Origins of Mass Opinion.* New York: Cambridge University Press.

———. 1996. "The Myth of Massive Media Impact Revived." In *Political Persuasion and Attitude Change,* ed. Diana C. Mutz, Paul M. Sniderman, and Richard A. Brody, 17–78. Ann Arbor: University of Michigan Press.

———. 2004. "Floating Voters in U.S. Presidential Elections, 1948–2000." In *Studies in Public Opinion: Attitudes, Nonattitudes, Measurement Error, and Change,* ed. Paul Sniderman and Willem E. Saris, 166–214. Princeton, N.J.: Princeton University Press.

Zhao, Xinshu, and Steven H. Chaffee. 1995. "Campaign Advertisements versus Television News as Sources of Political Issue Information." *Public Opinion Quarterly* 59(1): 41–65.

Zukin, Cliff, and Robin Snyder. 1984. "Passive Learning: When the Media Environment Is the Message." *Public Opinion Quarterly* 48(3): 629–638.

Index

Abraham, Spencer, 52–53, 76
ad-tracking data, 9, 39–41
advertising exposure, impact on voter
    choice
  by emotional appeal, 93–99
  measurement of, 42–47
  by partisanship, 114–119
  by political knowledge, 107–114
  in presidential elections (2000 and
    2004), 54–59
  in presidential primaries (2000), 60–64
  in Senate elections (2000 and 2004),
    64–69
  trade-offs and imbalances, 72
"ad watches," 136–137
affective intelligence theory, 30
affect transfer model, 29–30, 88, 98
American National Election Studies (ANES)
  candidate evaluations, 47–48
  limitations of, 49
  persuasiveness of campaign advertising,
    14, 39, 55, 65, 88
  political information measurement,
    107–108
anger-focused ads, 84–87, 94–96, 98–99
Annenberg panel survey, 34
Ansolabehere, Stephen, 21–22, 34–35

Arceneaux, Kevin, 3, 33–34, 50
Associated Press, 126, 127

backlash, against negative ads
  model, 87–88
  risk of, 27–30
  in Senate vs. presidential elections, 94–
    96, 99–100
banner ads, 141–142
Berelson, Bernard, 34
blogs, 120
Bowles, Erskine, 70
Brader, Ted, 29, 30, 81
Bradley, Bill, 60–64
Brannon, Laura A., 34
Brigham Young University study. *See*
    BYU–UW survey
Brooks, Deborah Jordan, 29
Brown, Scott, 76
Burr, Richard, 70
Bush, George W.
  2000 election, 47, 48, 51, 54–59, 73–75,
    88–93
  2000 primaries, 60–64
  2004 election, 54–59, 73–75, 82, 85–86,
    88–99, 103–105, 107–119
  2004 primaries, 131

byproduct effects, 3, 22
Byrd, Robert, 52
BYU–UW survey
  candidate evaluation, 48
  persuasiveness of campaign advertising,
    14, 39–40, 55, 65, 88
  political knowledge, 53, 108

campaign advertising
  democratic accountability and, 149–152
  introduction, 1–6, 145–148
  online ads, 6–7, 120, 137–142, 150–151
  persuasiveness of (see persuasiveness of
    campaign advertising)
  positive-negative categorization of, 79–80
  role of, 16–18
  television (see television advertising)
campaign environment. See context, and
    persuasiveness of campaign adver-
    tising
campaign-finance law, 9–10
campaign issues, 121, 150
campaign reform initiatives, 17–18
candidate evaluations, advertising's
    impact on
  intended effects hypothesis, 27
  measurement of, 47–48, 55
  partisanship and, 114–119
  political knowledge and, 107–114
  presidential elections, 57, 98
Cantwell, Maria, 76
Carr, David, 8
Castor, Betty, 70, 76, 83, 95
CBS News, 51
CCES (Cooperative Congressional Elec-
    tion Study), 133
Chang, Chingching, 34
Chattanooga Times and Free Press, 125
Clinton, Hillary, 2, 17
Clinton, Joshua, 50
CNN, 105
Coburn, Tom, 84
cognitive accounts, 28
Coleman, Norm, 76
Colorado Senate race (2004), 70
competitiveness of campaign, 23, 25–26,
    53, 66–69

congressional elections
  2000, 92
  2004, 44–47, 69–71, 82–87, 88–90, 92,
    93–99, 107–119
  2006, viii, 124, 133–137
  2010, viii
  ad effectiveness, 52–53, 64–69
  ad tone impact, 88–90, 92
  county-level analysis, 73, 76–77
  data sources, 39–41
  media coverage of ads, 128–129
  number of ads per media market, 10–11
  voters' awareness of candidates, 23–24
consumer purchasing behavior, 12–13
context, and persuasiveness of campaign
    advertising, 51–78
  county-level effects, 71–77
  early vs. late timing, 69–71
  factors in, 23–26
  future research needs, 148–149
  introduction, 51–54
  in presidential elections, 54–59
  in presidential primary elections, 60–64
contrast ads, persuasiveness of
  media coverage and, 130
  methodological issues, 28–29, 80
  partisanship and, 35
  presidential elections, 64, 84, 90, 92
  Senate races, 92, 99
Cooperative Congressional Election Study
    (CCES), 133
Coors, Pete, 70
Corker, Bob, 124
corporations, campaign advertising
    spending, 7
county-level analysis, 71–77

data and research design, 37–50
  ad persuasion analysis, 14–16
  advertising exposure estimation, 42–47
  dependent variables and model specifi-
    cation, 47–49
  future needs, 148–149
  introduction, 37–39
  surveys and ad-tracking data, 39–41
Dean, Howard, 10, 131
democratic accountability, 149–152

Democratic Party
   2004 Senate ads, 44
   2008 election ads, 12
   campaign advertising sponsorship, 1–2
   negativity of ads, 3–4
   See also congressional elections; presidential election campaigns
Democrats, 34, 106, 114–119, 121
dependent variables, 47–49
direct mail, 36
discrete emotions model, 29–30, 88, 98
dosage-resistance model, of political awareness, 31–32
Dukakis, Michael, 2
DVRs (digital video recorders), 8

Edwards, John, 79
effectiveness of campaign advertising. *See* persuasiveness of campaign advertising
e-mails, 120
emotional appeals, ad effectiveness impact, 79–101
   future research needs, 148
   introduction, 79–80
   methodology of study, 81
   models, 87–88
   results of study, 93–101
   timing and frequency, 81–87
emotions, of voters, 28, 29–30, 88
enthusiasm-focused ads, 84–87, 96–98
environment, campaign. *See* context, and persuasiveness of campaign advertising
exposure to advertising. *See* advertising exposure, impact on voter choice

factual misrepresentations, 17, 150–151
fear ads, 82–87, 94–96, 98–99
Florida
   presidential election (2000), 75
   Senate race (2004), 70, 76, 83, 95
Ford, Harold, 124–125, 132
Fox, Michael J., 137–138
Fox News, 105
Franken, Al, 76
Freedman, Paul, 38
Fridkin, Kim L., 27

Gallaher, David, 52
Gallup poll, 3–4, 104
Gaudet, Hazel, 34
Geer, John G., 29, 113, 124, 150
general elections. *See* presidential election campaigns
Goldstein, Ken, 38
Google ads, 141–142
Gore, Al
   2000 election campaign, 47, 48, 51, 54–59, 73–75, 88–93
   2000 primaries, 60–64
Gorton, Slade, 76
gubernatorial campaigns, media coverage of ads, 129

Hagen, Michael G., 56
Hais, Michael, 6
Hillygus, D. Sunshine, 121
Hindman, Matthew, 140–141
Hitwise, 139
Holbert, R. Lance, 35
Horton, Willie, 2, 123
House elections. *See* congressional elections
Huber, Gregory, 3, 33–34, 50
Huckabee, Mike, 138
Hutchings, Vincent L., 33

imagery, 148
incumbents, 24, 53, 68, 96
independents, 34–35, 106, 114–119
intended effects model, 27, 87, 99–100
Internet
   campaign advertising, 6–7, 120, 137–142, 150–151
   campaign donations via, 10
Iyengar, Shanto, 21–22, 34–35

Jamieson, Kathleen Hall, 56
Jeffords, James, 76
Johnson, Lyndon, "Daisy Girl" ad, 123
Johnston, Richard, 56

Kaid, Lynda Lee, 27
Kaminski, Kelly, 35
Kaye, Kate, 7, 142
Kenney, Patrick J., 27

Kerry, John
  2004 campaign manager, 12
  2004 election campaign ads, 54–59, 73–
    75, 82, 85–86, 88–99, 103–105, 107–119
  Swift Boat Veterans for Truth contro-
    versy, 2, 17, 104–105, 106, 123
Knowledge Network, 50
Krosnick, Jon A., 34
Kurtz, Howard, 131

laboratory experiments, 14, 37, 38–39
Lau, Richard B., 27–28, 38
Lazarsfeld, Paul F., 34
Louden, Michael, 136

Martinez, Mel, 76, 95
McCain, John
  2008 election campaign, viii, 7, 12, 16,
    23–24, 75–76, 131, 138–140
  2008 primaries, 60–64
McCaskill, Claire, 138
McGinnis, Joe, 12
McMahon, Steve, 27
media coverage of ads, 123–143
  Internet's influence, 137–142
  introduction, 123–124
  media-candidate relationship and, 130–
    132
  methodological issues, 130
  persuasive power of, 132–137
  reasons for, 129
  Tennessee "Harold, call me" ad, 124–
    125, 132
  trends, 126–129
media fragmentation, 7
media markets, defined, 9
Minnesota Senate race (2008), 76
Moveon.org, 105
MSNBC, 105
Murray, Patty, 95
music, 148
The Myth of Digital Democracy (Hindman), 140–141

NAES (National Annenberg Election
  Survey), 39, 50, 60
"nano-targeting," 141

National Annenberg Election Survey
  (NAES), 39, 50, 60
National Republican Senatorial Committee (NRSC), 124
negative ads
  backlash against, 27–30, 87–88, 94–96,
    99–100
  definition issues, 79–80
  Hillary Clinton's "3 A.M." ad, 2, 17
  issues mentioned in, 150
  media coverage, 130
  persuasiveness of, 26–28, 38, 151–152
  public opinion of, 3–4
  Swift Boat Veterans for Truth ads, 2, 17,
    104–105, 106, 123
  in Tennessee Senate race (2006), 124–
    125, 132
  timing and frequency of, 81–87
  voter turnout impact, 21–22
  Willie Horton ads, 2, 123
Nethercutt, George, 95
newspapers. See media coverage of ads
New York Times
  ad-related coverage trends, 127
  Swift Boat Veterans ad coverage, 105
  television ads, 8
  Tennessee Senate race (2006) coverage,
    124, 125
  Willie Horton ads, 2
Nielsen, 7–8
Nixon, Richard, 12
North Carolina Senate race (2004), 70
NRSC (National Republican Senatorial
  Committee), 124

Obama, Barack
  2008 election, viii, 7, 12, 16, 23–24, 75–
    76, 131, 138–140
  2008 primaries, 2, 9, 10, 17, 64
  fundraising efforts, 7, 10
  website traffic, 139–140
  "Yes, We Can" ad, 138
online advertising
  factual misrepresentations, 150–151
  future of, 6, 120
  Obama campaign fundraising, 7
  persuasiveness of, 137–142

political knowledge and, 120
political knowledge of viewers and,
    140–141
open-seat races, 24–25, 53, 68
Owen, Andrew, 50

partisanship, 34–35, 106, 114–119, 120–
    122
Penn, Mark, 2
Perdue, Bob, 17
personal appearances by candidates, 48
persuasiveness of campaign advertising
    ad characteristics and, 28–30, 79–101
    context and, 23–26, 51–78
    data and research design, 14–16, 37–50,
        148–149
    future research issues, 148–149
    limitations of study, 35–36
    literature review, 21–23
    media coverage and, 123–143
    methodology of study, 14–16
    online advertising, 137–142
    positive vs. negative ads, 151–152
    receivers' characteristics, 31–35, 103–
        122
Pfau, Michael, 35, 136
Pinkleton, Bruce E., 27
Polimetrix, 133
political issues, 121, 150
political knowledge, 31–34, 107–114, 120,
    140–141
Pomper, Gerald M., 27
presidential election campaigns
    1968, 12
    1988, 2
    2000, 47, 48, 51, 54–59, 73–75, 88–93
    2004, 2, 17, 54–59, 69–71, 73–75, 82–86,
        88–99, 103–105, 107–119
    2008, viii, 7, 12, 16, 23–24, 75–76, 131
    ad persuasiveness, 51, 54–59, 69–71,
        73–75, 107–119
    ad tone impact, 88–93
    county-level analysis, 73–77
    data sources, 39–41
    number of ads per media market, 11–12
    voters' awareness of candidates, 23,
        107–119

presidential nomination campaigns
    2000, 60–64
    2004, 9, 10, 131
    2008, 2, 9, 10, 17, 64
    ad persuasiveness, 60–64
    number of ads per media market, 8–9
press releases, 131–132
Price, Vincent, 107
public opinion polls, 3–4, 104

Rather, Dan, 103
receivers' characteristics, and ad effective-
    ness, 103–122
    future research needs, 148–149
    introduction, 103–107
    partisanship, 34–35, 114–119
    political knowledge, 31–34, 107–114
    results of study, 120–122
Republican Party
    2004 Senate ads, 44
    campaign advertising sponsorship,
        1–2
    consumer purchasing data use, 12–13
    negativity of ads, 3–4
    See also congressional elections; presi-
        dential election campaigns
Republicans, 34, 106, 114–119, 121
research methodology. See data and
    research design
Romney, Mitt, 79
Rovner, Ivy Brown, 27–28, 38

Salazar, Ken, 70
search ads, 141–142
Senate elections. See congressional
    elections
Shields, Todd G., 121
Shrum, Bob, 12
Sigelman, Lee, 27–28, 38
60 Minutes, 103–104
Stabenow, Debbie, 52–53, 76
state-level presidential advertising, 22
State of the Union address, 7
stem-cell research, 121, 137–138
Stevens, Daniel, 43
Stone, Roger, 26–27
survey data, 14, 39–41

Swift Boat Veterans for Truth ads, 2, 17, 104–105, 106, 123
Szabo, Erin A., 35

targeting, 12–13, 36, 141
television advertising
    factual misrepresentations in, 17, 150
    length of, 113–114
    persuasiveness of, 33–34
    relevance of, 6–13
    role of, 16–18
television viewing habits, 7–8, 43
Tennessee Senate race (2006), 124–125, 132
timing of advertising, 25, 53, 69–71
tone of advertising, 26–30, 82–84, 88–93, 101. *See also* negative ads

UCLA, Cooperative Congressional Election Study, 133
unions, campaign advertising spending, 7
University of Wisconsin
    Cooperative Congressional Election Study, 133
    NewsLab, 134
    See also BYU–UW survey

Valentino, Nicholas A., 33
voter characteristics. *See* receivers' characteristics, and ad effectiveness
voter persuasion. *See* persuasiveness of campaign advertising
voter turnout, 21–22

Washington Post, 124, 125, 126–127, 131
Washington Senate race (2000), 76
Wattenberg, Martin, 7
wedge issues, 121
West, Darrell M., 126
Wicker, Tom, 2
Williams, Dimitri, 33
Willie Horton ads, 2, 123
Winograd, Morley, 6
Wisconsin Advertising Project, 8–9, 14, 40, 81, 124, 134

"Yes, We Can" ad, 138
YouTube, 125, 137–138

Zaller, John, 31, 72, 107

TRAVIS N. RIDOUT is Associate Professor of Political Science at Washington State University and a coauthor (with Michael M. Franz, Paul B. Freedman, and Kenneth M. Goldstein) of *Campaign Advertising and American Democracy* (Temple).

MICHAEL M. FRANZ is Associate Professor of Government and Legal Studies at Bowdoin College, author of *Choices and Changes: Interest Groups in the Electoral Process,* and a coauthor (with Paul B. Freedman, Kenneth M. Goldstein, and Travis N. Ridout) of *Campaign Advertising and American Democracy* (Temple).